KB136861

Vitamin New Toeic Voca

Vitamin New Toeic Voca

조동인 지음

도서출판 동인

Preface

영어 학습에 있어 기본이 되는 것은 어휘이다. 문장이 의미 전달을 위한 그릇이라면 그 문장 안에 담기는 어휘는 그릇에 담기는 재료와 같다. 재료가 좋으면 음식의 맛이 좋은 것처럼 풍부하고 깊은 어휘력은 듣기와 말하기, 읽기와 쓰기의 영역에서 의미 전달의 깊이와 내용을 풍성하게 해준다. 여기 2016년 5월부터 새로 바뀐 토익 유형에 맞춘 새로운 내용의 풍성한 어휘들을 준비하였다. 단순한 암기가 아닌 효율적인 어휘 학습을 위해 part5의 문제 형식으로 책을 썼다. 많은 학생들이 본 교재로 열심히 학습하여 새로 바뀐 정기 토익에서 좋은 결실을 맺길 기원하는 바이다.

2016년 7월 20일
저자 올림

Contents

문제편

Vitamin New Toeic Voca

001. Andy Martin ltd. _____ with Jason Chemicals Inc. next upcoming January to be a conglomerate.

(A) merger
(B) merged
(C) is going to merge
(D) has merged

002. Before we take care of the final bidding, we should double check _____ numbers and numerical analysis.

(A) ourselves
(B) ours
(C) our
(D) us

003. The Metropolitan arts exhibition consists of _____ paintings and artifacts by many municipal artists and residents.

(A) when
(B) or
(C) if
(D) both

004. A _____ version of Mr. Markerson's book will be sent to the chief editor for the next month publication.

(A) revise

(B) revised

(C) revising

(D) revision

005. Be sure to _____ the notice which contains essential information concerning reshuffle of personnel to every employee.

(A) distribute

(B) distributed

(C) to distribute

(D) to be distributed

006. Maxim and Maxima International Champions attracted a _____ of 200 guests with paid admission for the performance.

(A) goal

(B) total

(C) final

(D) purpose

007. The number of visitors to Jason & Jamie Cosmetics' web site has tripled _____ a year.

(A) within
(B) out of
(C) at
(D) then

008. When listing _____ on your application, you should refer to exact titles and specific dates.

(A) accomplishing
(B) accomplished
(C) accomplishments
(D) accomplish

009. During the promotional _____ the customers who pay a visit to Macy's department store in New York can get more discount rate.

(A) shop
(B) period
(C) part
(D) authority

010. After continuous trial and error Nelson Independent Chemicals has floated _____ its company on the stock market.

(A) successful
(B) successively
(C) successfully
(D) succession

011. With newly launched mobile phones gaining popularity, you will find _____ for sale at many off line stores as well as online.

(A) they
(B) their
(C) them
(D) themselves

012. Motorists are _____ recommended to drive with much care especially at night on the wet roads.

(A) strongly
(B) strength
(C) strong
(D) stronger

013. The Canadian prime minister, John Mcguill raised more _____ two million dollars for environmental protection and reducing co2 gas.

(A) than
(B) as
(C) even
(D) over

014. Maria and Marion Enterprise Inc. specialize in military database by _____ solutions and security in case of hacking.

(A) provide
(B) provides
(C) provided
(D) providing

015. Despite several times of distribution of information, many employees were _____ of operating security system.

(A) willing
(B) sensitive
(C) unaware
(D) undesirable

016. All forms of payment _____ cyber money can be accepted and circulated on the game web site, DigiMon.

    (A) at

    (B) toward

    (C) of

    (D) including

017. The _____ features of LX 12 mobile phone are its unique information security and speedy process of text messages.

    (A) distinctly

    (B) distinctive

    (C) distinction

    (D) distinctively

018. Most of the critics in the modern arts officially _____ that Angela's some paintings are forgery by the European Arts Appraisal Association.

    (A) promote

    (B) cite

    (C) craft

    (D) argue

019. Jason McMillan officially heard that she got _____ time to submit her application for the job opening in search of an accountant.

   (A) about
   (B) next
   (C) still
   (D) ever

020. Of all the applicants seeking the job of accountant, Mr. Giambee is viewed as the _____.

   (A) qualification
   (B) most qualified
   (C) qualified
   (C) more qualified

021. _____ your annual donations are not overdue, you are supposed to take all the rights as a patron of Pederson Foundations.

   (A) But
   (B) In case of
   (C) As long as
   (D) Rather than

022. The breathtaking mountainous view is the _____ many tourists come to Switzerland all the year round.

(A) reasonable
(B) reasoning
(C) reasoned
(D) reason

023. The prime minister contributed significantly to _____ his country as the superpower in Europe.

(A) rebuilds
(B) rebuilding
(C) rebuilt
(D) being rebuilt

024. Mark Pierson Inc. offers a wide range of _____ quality display gadgets in the country.

(A) afford
(B) affordable
(C) affording
(D) affords

025. Martin Kensington, _____ marketing strategy, is very effective to the target customers, is going to deliver a keynote speech at the conference.

(A) whom
(B) what
(C) which
(D) whose

026. Miller Klarkson _____ the direction of famous legend singer Michael Kimberly will be performing a live concert tonight.

(A) to
(B) under
(C) around
(D) at

027. Promoting sales and inviting customers from New York _____ due to severe rainfalls and unstable weather.

(A) postponed
(B) is postponing
(C) will postpone
(D) was postponed

028. After _____ investment in production capacity, Miller Brewers has increased its revenue by 20 percent.

(A) substantial

(B) substance

(C) substantially

(D) substantiate

029. You should _____ to the changes not to have any damage on your computer network.

(A) promote

(B) undo

(C) revert

(D) boot

030. *Time* magazine as well as *Newsweek* will go through _____ transformation from print to electronic.

(A) publication

(B) undecided

(C) representation

(D) contribution

031. The _____ atmosphere of Kommpson co. promotes more productivity in spite of tension between workers.

    (A) competitiveness
    (B) compete
    (C) competitive
    (D) competitor

032. Thanks to his _____ for the revival of industrial city, Malcome Jackson was able to run for mayor election.

    (A) patronizing
    (B) patronizes
    (C) patronage
    (D) patronized

033. Security system is the top _____ in the cyber space and internet environment in the world.

    (A) privacy
    (B) priority
    (C) premium
    (D) product

034. New employee training program was composed of teaching and practice by much _____ staff members.

    (A) experienced
    (B) experience
    (C) experiencing
    (D) experiences

035. It was the third _____ month of sales increases, while production had its biggest rise in 15 months.

    (A) being consecutive
    (B) consecutive
    (C) consecutively
    (D) being consecutively

036. The company will sharply _____ production of A 12, its most expensive smart phone as demand on premium mobile phones dwindles.

    (A) curtail
    (B) cutting
    (C) cuts
    (D) curtails

037. Meridian Hamilton Inc. would need to significantly _____ its production and shave operating costs due to economic slowdown.

(A) streamline
(B) start
(C) strike
(D) stick

038. The company _____ its centennial on Thursday with plans to sharpen its focus on innovation and ambitious enterprises for supersonic commercial flight.

(A) marking
(B) marked
(C) marker
(D) to mark

039. Mr. Markerson all the time _____ to recognize and admire the individual achievements of his team members in the company.

(A) talks
(B) thinks
(C) strives
(D) focuses

040. _____ purchase of Airbus A380 with the largest seating capacity, the final decision from the board of directors should be made.

(A) By
(B) Prior to
(C) Since
(D) Into

041. Kempton International Catering announces that the company will release _____ brand new salad dishes this year.

(A) custom
(B) customized
(C) customs
(D) custom

042. Melany Kahill was _____ as the journalist of the year with the article on the upcoming mayor election.

(A) naming
(B) names
(C) named
(D) name

043. You'd better upgrade your contactable information _____ submitting your application for the job opening.

   (A) to
   (B) before
   (C) at
   (D) within

044. Amid increasing _____, the IT company made a lot of efforts to develop innovative items.

   (A) competition
   (B) competitive
   (C) competitiveness
   (D) compete

045. All _____ will take place at Grand Multipurpose Stage in the heart of New York City.

   (A) perform
   (B) performer
   (C) performs
   (D) performances

046. The repairman will _____ a close inspection of any defected parts in the production line.

 (A) look
 (B) repair
 (C) conduct
 (D) search

047. Top Celestial Inc. tries to employ _____ staff and to promote potentials of the workers.

 (A) diversify
 (B) diversely
 (C) diversity
 (D) diverse

048. Matt Motors is _____ to developing electric cars for the purpose of pursuing harmless and clean fuel of the car.

 (A) committed
 (B) commits
 (C) committing
 (D) commit

049. Mark Jacob volunteered to give a hand to the department of customer service _____ he had never worked for the department.

(A) despite
(B) in spite
(C) although
(D) even

050. _____ the fact that Taster's Coffee Brewers are available online, most of the customers purchase them from the stores.

(A) Though
(B) Even though
(C) In spite
(D) Despite

051. From candles to jewelry, Melike's Boutique has the perfect gift for any _____.

(A) occasioned
(B) occasional
(C) occasion
(D) occasionally

052. Dr. Cabot intends to replace the furniture in the meeting room to make it more _____ for patients.

(A) comfortable
(B) reachable
(C) probable
(D) capable

053. Because the CEO's statements were not quoted _____, the interview must be revised before the publication.

(A) corrects
(B) correctly
(C) correcting
(D) correction

054. The building contractors offered the Kelstham Electrical the same contract terms _____ were offered to them last year.

(A) whose
(B) when
(C) that
(D) they

055. The author revealed that the ideas from her novels were drawn _____ from her experiences growing up in Spain.

(A) ideally
(B) largely
(C) seemingly
(D) probably

056. The events committee _____ requested that Cherman's Caterers provide the food for this year's holiday party.

(A) specifics
(B) specified
(C) specifically
(D) specified

057. Ms. Wordington _____ the keynote speech at the Vision in Ecotourism convention.

(A) delivered
(B) achieved
(C) pursued
(D) implied

058. Same-day-delivery can be scheduled _____ you place your order before 10 A.M.

(A) if
(B) for
(C) yet
(D) either

059. The Gregston Hotel's flexibility regarding check-in time is an _____ of its commitment to customer satisfaction.

(A) indicating
(B) indicative
(C) indication
(D) identified

060. Some seats are still available in the third row for the people who want a closer _____ of the stage.

(A) view
(B) sight
(C) watch
(D) show

061. Players around the world are in search of rare and valuable game items and connect _____ each other.

(A) once
(B) then
(C) with
(D) just

062. The municipal chief director in transportation said that the _____ challenge is that the city should construct subway stations.

(A) significance
(B) signifier
(C) significantly
(D) most significant

063. _____ waste of fossil fuel during production has caused air pollution and the health problem among the staffs.

(A) Sure
(B) A lot
(C) Many
(D) Excessive

064. Peli and Keli clothing store is very fashionable and popular among customers because it is attractive and _____ priced.

(A) affordably
(B) affordability
(C) affording
(D) affords

065. Manhattan General Hospital is reliable, since it employs the _____ doctors from the many medical fields.

(A) qualification
(B) qualifies
(C) quality
(D) qualified

066. Neither the price _____ the quality of the smart phone GK15 is satisfying mobile phone users.

(A) with
(B) nor
(C) or
(D) though

067. Due to _____ layoff large number of employees in the sales department left the company.

    (A) invalid
    (B) massive
    (C) void
    (D) vacant

068. Be sure to bring your _____ receipts when requesting reimbursement for travel expenses.

    (A) signed
    (B) signs
    (C) singing
    (D) to sign

069. Law _____ on illegally imported building materials was announced in order to prevent any smuggler.

    (A) supplies
    (B) recruitment
    (C) enforcement
    (D) authorities

070. _____ the CEO, the managing director announced that the company is going to merge with another IT company.

(A) Provided that

(B) Because

(C) Between

(D) On behalf of

071. By means of shaving the costs, the company is heavily depending _____ the assistance from the volunteers around the world.

(A) among

(B) on

(C) up

(D) into

072. Even though other seats in the airplane remain empty during the flight you should not _____ them.

(A) occupancy

(B) approach

(C) occupy

(D) approaching

073. For the purpose of security _____ at the production line, all the workers should wear identification badges.

(A) being enhanced
(B) to enhance
(C) enhancement
(D) enhanced

074. The MTV provides full _____ of Academy Awards in 2016 at Channel 25 tonight.

(A) coverage
(B) curtailing
(C) cut
(D) cushion

075. _____ Mr. Markerson tried to play the augmented-reality game like Pokemon Go, he could not enjoy it well due to connection delay.

(A) Despite
(B) Eventually
(C) In spite
(D) Even though

076. Today a featured speaker on auto industry will _____ cyber security in mobile phones.

  (A) address
  (B) talk
  (C) envelop
  (D) inspect

077. Among the contenders for the best actor Mr. Parker _____ the prize of Actor of the Year.

  (A) awarding
  (B) was awarded
  (C) awarded
  (D) having awarded

078. Despite the spirited discussion concerning increase in overtime payment, the management could not _____ it.

  (A) finalize
  (B) deal
  (C) tell
  (D) talk to

079. The foreign company, Nintenda nowadays _____ in a video game which makes use of augmented-reality.

    (A) specialists
    (B) specialty
    (C) specializes
    (D) specializing

080. Many analysts in Europe will consider how banks are _____ the so-called Brexit vote.

    (A) responded
    (B) responds
    (C) respondent
    (D) responding to

081. You'd better be _____ that the smart phone you ordered from our online web site is no longer available.

    (A) advise
    (B) advice
    (C) advised
    (D) advises

082. Employees should _____ not to use the main photocopier at the supply room until the machine is fixed.

(A) be parted
(B) be informed
(C) be attended
(D) be respected

083. Manfred Peterson serves as a courier service manager in New York branch for _____ years without a break.

(A) conducting
(B) confined
(C) consecutive
(D) conformed

084. At the end of this year our CEO will _____ special training course for the newly employed staffs.

(A) introduced
(B) introduce
(C) introductory
(D) introductions

085. The _____ file specifies details of the company policy concerning sales enhancement.

    (A) attachment
    (B) attached
    (C) attach
    (D) attaching

086. All the newly employed staffs will receive a/an _____ card to pass the gates and get security.

    (A) identification
    (B) handbook
    (C) partition
    (D) parking

087. The CEOs of the two companies emphasized that both of them secured _____ the economic partnership.

    (A) tradition
    (B) traditional
    (C) traditionally
    (D) traditionalize

088. The tycoon of the company demanded _____ information regarding how to develop augmented-reality programs from the department of R&D.

   (A) details

   (B) detailing

   (C) detailed

   (D) detail

089. The cyber security program has been installed to prevent any _____ hacking and online terrors.

   (A) hazardous

   (B) lucrative

   (C) beneficial

   (D) dependent

090. The CEO of the company _____ that M&A with Jason Miller Inc. will bring much more benefits in the forseeable future.

   (A) scheduled

   (B) assured

   (C) parted

   (D) inserted

091. The company said that its _____ in the first quarter rose 15 percent due to the countless efforts for sales promotion.

    (A) revenue
    (B) part
    (C) market
    (D) schedule

092. The _____ scenes of the mountain are famous tourist spot and are attracting many visitors around the world.

    (A) remarking
    (B) remarkable
    (C) remarkably
    (D) remark

093. _____ the cost estimate, the building renovation is expected to cost another one million dollars.

    (A) Aside from
    (B) Next to
    (C) Instead of
    (D) Out of

094. Thanks to outstanding job performance of the sales team, the company is expected to _____ the contract with the sales manger.

(A) extends
(B) extension
(C) extend
(D) extending

095. It is predicted that consumer price index will increase _____ 30 and 35 percent compared to last year's.

(A) between
(B) both
(C) either
(D) about

096. The _____ of governmental development funds is quite crucial, since revenue and expenditure should be balanced.

(A) allocating
(B) allocate
(C) allocates
(D) allocation

097. It is urgently _____ that all the employees should bring their ID cards in order to enter the office.

    (A) require
    (B) requires
    (C) required
    (D) requirement

098. For your summer leave the department of general affairs demands that you should get _____ from your supervisor in advance.

    (A) the sign
    (B) the signature
    (C) the signing
    (D) the signs

099. The department of public relations is already trying to _____ an ad of recruitment in the newspaper.

    (A) tell
    (B) demand
    (C) placement
    (D) put

100. The department of information and security announces that unnecessary data _____ is prohibited especially when you are at the desk.

(A) retrieved

(B) retrieval

(C) retrieving

(D) retrieve

101. _____ repeated changes in leadership and strategy Mall & Shoppers Inc. is leading produce circulation in the U.S.

(A) Despite

(B) In spite

(C) Dues

(D) For

102. The Baby and Johnson ltd. gives the customers refunds only _____ they bring their receipts.

(A) which

(B) how

(C) that

(D) when

103. Due to the _____ characteristics of M&A details of it will not be informed to the third parties.

    (A) appropriate
    (B) effective
    (C) careful
    (D) sensitive

104. Green Plastic Inc. provides customers with fresh fruits from the _____ farms all the year round.

    (A) previous
    (B) local
    (C) region
    (D) exact

105. In spite of _____ reviews, many consumers count on online information on the ratings of restaurants.

    (A) compound
    (B) fraudulent
    (C) magnificent
    (D) agile

106. The recruitment for the job opening will not proceed for a
_____ due to complaints by some applicants.

(A) stay
(B) break
(C) session
(D) while

107. The National Charity Foundation aids children of the disabled
_____ subsidizing school tuition.

(A) from
(B) by
(C) to
(D) of

108. Marilyn Inc. specializes in _____ of identity design of a
company to satisfy clients' demand.

(A) create
(B) creates
(C) creatively
(D) creativeness

109. The board of directors approved of remodeling of the hotel to _____ room capacity to satisfy customers' demand.

   (A) maximize
   (B) specialize
   (C) hold
   (D) intend

110. Supervisors are in _____ of advising their juniors especially when they don't know the direction of the company.

   (A) care
   (B) charge
   (C) chance
   (D) change

111. The management considers that shaving production costs is a top _____ in times of economic slowdown.

   (A) check
   (B) pride
   (C) priority
   (D) crisis

112. Bulgaria is famous _____ its inexpensive lodging, fantastic seafood, and gorgeous beaches in the Black Sea.

   (A) with
   (B) for
   (C) at
   (D) to

113. According to travel magazine _____ travelers try to save money by using cheap flights and lodging.

   (A) frugal
   (B) economic
   (C) lavish
   (D) intuitive

114. It was true that the company was _____ over 100 years ago, when the present chairman was not born.

   (A) sent
   (B) established
   (C) originated
   (D) took place

115. According to the comments of my _____ Martin Perez is one of the leading consultants in the field of M&A.

    (A) adviser
    (B) advice
    (C) advising
    (D) advised

116. The air conditioner of High Tech Development consumes about 50 percent less electricity than _____ products.

    (A) reasonable
    (B) part
    (C) economic
    (D) conventional

117. The sunny hot weather of the region enabled many vineyards to harvest high _____ grapes for wine this year.

    (A) quality
    (B) quantity
    (C) qualities
    (D) quantities

118. Many motorists suffered from ill information, since detour signs were not _____ posted.

    (A) adequate
    (B) adequately
    (C) affluent
    (D) affluently

119. The executive director responded _____ to assistant manager's business proposal than anyone else.

    (A) being positive
    (B) positively
    (C) more positively
    (D) most positive

120. It is said that the main branch will be renovated next year _____ the approval by the board of directors.

    (A) in case of
    (B) provided that
    (C) in addition to
    (D) as a sign of

121. According to the newspapers many parents wondered at what age they should give their child full _____ to smart phones.

    (A) access
    (B) path
    (C) key
    (D) route

122. In order to give a hand to charity foundation take a _____ to fill out the survey paper.

    (A) check
    (B) part
    (C) moment
    (D) look

123. For the negotiation of pay increase your last year's signed _____ must be brought with.

    (A) contract
    (B) contraction
    (C) contractor
    (D) contracting

124. Common Sense Media polled over 1000 parents in the street found that there was no _____ guideline for children's use of internet.

    (A) specification
    (B) specify
    (C) specifies
    (D) specific

125. The _____ guest for the music program received a warm welcome from the audience on the floor.

    (A) feature
    (B) featured
    (C) features
    (D) featuring

126. The car's financing program and residual value buyback program will reduce the total costs of _____ the vehicle.

    (A) owned
    (B) owns
    (C) owner
    (D) owning

127. _____ by the city council members at the municipal conference was unexpectedly high.

(A) Attendants
(B) Attends
(C) Attendees
(D) Attendance

128. The restaurant was awarded the Clean and Safe Prize due to the servers' regular check to get rid of chemical _____ in vegetables and food supplies.

(A) residues
(B) residing
(C) residence
(D) resign

129. According to Medical Times many people are _____ of their acid reflux from stomach.

(A) with danger
(B) danger
(C) risk
(D) at risk

130. Jason Markakis had to put his job on _____ due to the late response from his boss yesterday.

   (A) hole
   (B) hell
   (C) hold
   (D) home

131. This year's book award recipient, Tabitha Orland, will _____ by her editor, Margo Zeller.

   (A) introduce
   (B) be introduced
   (C) be introducing
   (D) have introduced

132. Owing to the high demand for our products, Belwald Footwear shipments may be delayed by _____ days.

   (A) several
   (B) plentiful
   (C) hopeful
   (D) other

133. To be eligible for research grants, applicants must be certified engineers in the country in _____ they reside.

    (A) which
    (B) where
    (C) from
    (D) there

134. Melnar Furnishings allows customers to _____ their bills into five easy monthly payments.

    (A) divide
    (B) reserve
    (C) number
    (D) substitute

135. We have received an overwhelming _____ to our call for nominees for this year's Employee Award.

    (A) responsive
    (B) response
    (C) responded
    (D) respond

136. Rain can cause a baseball game to be delayed or canceled _____ the field becomes too wet.

(A) or
(B) until
(C) if
(D) and

137. With the rise of online sales, consumers leave home to shop much less _____ than in the past.

(A) frequency
(B) frequent
(C) frequently
(D) frequence

138. By the end of today's workshop, you will be _____ in using the upgraded software.

(A) legitimate
(B) proficient
(C) practical
(D) official

139. When your application is approved, you will receive your new credit card by mail _____ one week.

    (A) once
    (B) since
    (C) while
    (D) within

140. It is of little surprise that social, outgoing employees work better _____ teams than alone.

    (A) without
    (B) in
    (C) at
    (D) over

141. The company has tried to increase _____ force by 50 percent in the first quarter for the large revenue this year.

    (A) sells
    (B) sold
    (C) sales
    (D) salable

142. The _____ gear of the car KC12 has vastly increased reported crashes and motorists' injuries.

(A) fault
(B) faulty
(C) faulted
(D) faults

143. There were floral _____ in every corner of the street and even in the square for the feast of the city.

(A) excellence
(B) presentation
(C) responsibility
(D) arrangements

144. The McMillan Consulting Inc. consults only professional groups _____ the Law Association, and Trusty Management Ltd.

(A) such as
(B) given
(C) because
(D) whether

145. For your cyber security the TS App on your smart phone needs
to _____ safety function first.

(A) acknowledge
(B) accomplish
(C) implement
(D) extend

146. The duty of the factory manager is to _____ the production of
metal parts on a regular basis.

(A) please
(B) resolve
(C) secure
(D) contain

147. Passengers with first-class tickets will _____ a plane first and
enjoy quality service in the cabin during the flight.

(A) boards
(B) on board
(C) boarding
(D) board

148. The Markerson Millan Corporate's ill _____ produces bad results and soaring complaints from the workers.

(A) managers
(B) manages
(C) management
(D) manage

149. _____ location of Maritime Hotel is one of its strengths to the guests who frequently use the subway in New York.

(A) Convenient
(B) Convenience
(C) Conveniences
(D) Conveniently

150. Nowadays electric cars like Tesla are gaining popularity due to _____ of taxes and low maintenance costs.

(A) deducting
(B) deduct
(C) reduction
(D) reduce

151. The total cost of Highway 202 in Mid West will be more expensive, since the company's bid was _____ an estimate.

   (A) carefully
   (B) merely
   (C) modestly
   (D) enormously

152. As the _____ company succeeded beyond anyone's guess, the investment of half million turned into close to half a billion.

   (A) venture
   (B) vent
   (C) vend
   (D) vending

153. According to newest information source shortly after Poketmon Go was released it became a global _____.

   (A) sense
   (B) sensation
   (C) senses
   (D) sensing

154. At Global Charming Shampoo Inc, normal shipping is free of charge _____ the distance of delivery.

   (A) without
   (B) other than
   (C) along
   (D) regardless of

155. There are many convenient ways for sightseers to travel New York city _____ walking or driving.

   (A) instead
   (B) apart
   (C) except
   (D) rather

156. The company was at a loss since it was _____ from a real threat to online security from cyber terrorists.

   (A) knowing
   (B) suffering
   (C) seeing
   (D) taking

157. In the _____ future the venture capitalist expects to reap enormous revenue from his investment.

    (A) foreseeable
    (B) foresees
    (C) foreseeing
    (D) foresaw

158. Santanasoft offers technical support for all of its software products _____ its competitors only provide help for current releases.

    (A) unlike
    (B) whereas
    (C) as far as
    (D) in order that

159. If you want to make your dream come true, you should _____ implement your plans.

    (A) vigilantly
    (B) vigilant
    (C) vigilance
    (D) vigil

160. _____ concerns about rising living cost and monthly rent, the Association of National Housing Policy recommended a sharable house.

(A) Abroad

(B) Atop

(C) Amid

(D) Aside

161. The owner of Maritime Shipping Inc. announced that the company _____ price of M&A with another corporate.

(A) negotiation

(B) negotiates

(C) negotiability

(D) negotiable

162. Students can _____ access and enroll the professional online study program at the homepage.

(A) easily

(B) least

(C) very

(D) little

163. In the newspaper Macrobuilt Inc. announced that it had twelve _____ around the world.

    (A) subsidy
    (B) subsidiaries
    (C) sub
    (D) subsidiary

164. The billionaire and co-founder of internet messenger program is searching _____ next investment opportunities for the U.S. market.

    (A) for
    (B) by
    (C) at
    (D) to

165. Ushers at the theater will help the customers _____ their seats especially during the intermission.

    (A) make
    (B) locate
    (C) send
    (D) ask

166. Magic Purifier co. never turned a profit and the high debt _____ it to default on loans.

    (A) made
    (B) forced
    (C) got
    (D) tired

167. All tickets will be refunded _____ of the bad weather through the homepage of the soccer club.

    (A) provided
    (B) if
    (C) in case of
    (D) due

168. Many investors purchased the stocks of T&T Inc. despite the _____ that the company's earnings in the first quarter were lower than anticipated.

    (A) truth
    (B) fact
    (C) act
    (D) pact

169. A year and a half after the launch, the magazine _____ publication due to lack of readers' interest.

    (A) blocked
    (B) stopping
    (C) ceased
    (D) prevented

170. In the interview with the news press Mark Trumbo's success was mainly _____ on diligence, and passion.

    (A) rely
    (B) based
    (C) come
    (D) stayed

171. The Watertown Prunevill is _____ located just by a metro station which leads to the region's most attractive tourist spot.

    (A) conveniently
    (B) consistently
    (C) continually
    (D) commonly

172. You'd better be _____ of the detailed specifications before attempting to install PC vaccine program onto your notebook computer.

    (A) direct
    (B) review
    (C) informed
    (D) founded

173. The president's announcement was made during a one-day conference on "Security Research" _____ at the college.

    (A) held
    (B) hung
    (C) kept
    (D) seen

174. The host was _____ to announce the last winner of beauty pageant at the Grand Rexington Hall.

    (A) delighting
    (B) delighted
    (C) delights
    (D) delight

175. With its convenient public transportation and highly skilled workforce, Marion Valley is a very _____ location for IT companies.

    (A) offering
    (B) proposing
    (C) promising
    (D) identifying

176. History majors are attending the Metropolitan Museum in New York now that it _____ authentic Egyptian arts.

    (A) feature
    (B) features
    (C) featureless
    (D) featuring

177. Mr. Crawford is a board member of a nonprofit group _____ the Freedom of the Reporters.

    (A) calls
    (B) caller
    (C) call
    (D) called

178. The security team will be _____ for the information surveillance by CC TVs from diverse angles.

    (A) response
    (B) responsive
    (C) respond
    (D) responsible

179. The minister of education has a strong belief that education and learning should be a universal right and not a _____.

    (A) privilege
    (B) character
    (C) reputation
    (D) consequence

180. George Hughes, a famous geneticist who is exploring genetic engineering techniques to _____ extinct species.

    (A) revive
    (B) survive
    (C) involve
    (D) revolve

181. Miller Parkerson had signed over the _____ to his wife just before he experienced the car accident.

(A) permission
(B) property
(C) comparison
(D) registration

182. The company has not decided _____ how to deal with the unexpected rumors concerning its stocks.

(A) precise
(B) precision
(C) preciseness
(D) precisely

183. _____ all the preliminary interviews have been completed, only two applicants for the job opening will be contacted.

(A) During
(B) As soon as
(C) So that
(D) Despite

184. Chris Bryant and his partner should have consulted a business
_____ at the very moment of selling off his company.

(A) dealer
(B) party
(C) adviser
(D) shopper

185. Not only the sales manager but also his CEO was disappointed
with sales record _____ the summer vacation season.

(A) while
(B) beside
(C) during
(D) with

186. The CEO demanded that the sales manager should give him
more _____ ideas on sales promotion.

(A) specifics
(B) specify
(C) specific
(D) specifically

187. In times of economic boom, price is _____ to increase regardless of pay raise for workers.

(A) risen
(B) seen
(C) limited
(D) bound

188. According to the Medical News many patients in the U.S. are worried about _____ in health premiums.

(A) boom
(B) rise
(C) up
(D) upward

189. Based on current customer data, the company prepared for the warranty _____ or complaints.

(A) role
(B) power
(C) claims
(D) pay

190. More than 34 percent of the vehicle's owners have filed a
     _____ against the auto maker regarding the false fuel
     efficiency.

    (A) law
    (B) legal
    (C) allegation
    (D) lawsuit

191. The Business Weekly revealed that the IT company was hesitant
     to plan to _____ many new employees this year.

    (A) recruit
    (B) file
    (C) join
    (D) work

192. If your company wants to be successful in Canada, firstly it has
     to be developing a major product _____ the market.

    (A) leader
    (B) leading
    (C) leads
    (D) lead

어휘 실력 기르기

193. Marion & Pamela Cosmetics has announced that its profits this year will be lower due to _____ sales.

   (A) depreciated
   (B) deprived
   (C) determined
   (D) deterred

194. Game companies in the forseeable future should be trying to create more _____ programs for their users.

   (A) invalid
   (B) instinctive
   (C) innovative
   (D) intentional

195. Many IT companies will make 50 to 60% cuts in their work forces _____ the next few years in order to become more competitive.

   (A) at
   (B) about
   (C) over
   (D) with

196. Many people took into account the fact that solar energy could be a cheap _____ for fossil fuels long time ago.

(A) difference

(B) substitute

(C) replacing

(D) change

197. The prospect for a good job this year is very _____ according to my professor.

(A) depressive

(B) depressing

(C) depressed

(D) depression

198. The bids for skyscrapers in the heart of Seoul submitted by the construction companies _____ in a special safe.

(A) placing

(B) placed

(C) are placing

(D) were placed

199. The amusement park is not _____ for any accidents caused by carelessness of children's parents.

    (A) respecting
    (B) responsible
    (C) reasonable
    (D) retreating

200. _____ the efforts by the police to reduce criminals and crimes in the region, the results have been disappointing so far.

    (A) Although
    (B) Despite
    (C) In spite
    (D) Between

201. If you didn't have _____ knowledge of chemistry and physics, you cannot become a professor of military science.

    (A) an extensive
    (B) an extremely
    (C) an outbound
    (D) a prevalent

202. Many people are _____ to note that a lot of defectors from the North are settling down well in the South.

(A) surprised

(B) surprise

(C) surprises

(D) being surprising

203. High ranking officials in the government is going to have to account _____ the mishandling of the policies.

(A) to

(B) with

(C) for

(D) by

204. Due to the severe blizzard the airport _____ announced that it should urgently shut down.

(A) monitors

(B) authorities

(C) party

(D) forces

205. The managing director could not set up a _____ plan on how many products should be churned out.

(A) reasoning
(B) reasons
(C) reason
(D) reasonable

206. The delivery order was _____ a year after the Jackson Vill Food Inc. and its contractor re-established business relations.

(A) send
(B) made
(C) went
(D) transmitted

207. The managing director in Meter & Miles Corporation _____ with its counterpart on details of sales condition between two companies.

(A) recommends
(B) negotiates
(C) refers
(D) consults

208. The number of diesel cars on the road _____ increasing due to cheap fuel and fuel efficiency.

(A) are
(B) are being
(C) is
(D) is been

209. Thanks to the trip-cancellation policy, he could get a _____ on his air fare from the insurance company.

(A) bill
(B) money
(C) refund
(D) premium

210. Whether you're traveling domestically or _____, a travel insurance is necessary for yourself.

(A) apart
(B) anytime
(C) alone
(D) abroad

해답편

Vitamin New Toeic Voca

001. Andy Martin ltd. _____ with Jason Chemicals Inc. next upcoming January to be a conglomerate.

   (A) merger
   (B) merged
   (C) is going to merge
   (D) has merged

정답) C

해설) upcoming 다가오는   conglomerate 대기업

merge는 타동사와 자동사 둘 다 가능하나 여기서는 자동사임.

merge with~ ~와 합병하다

The two companies were merged into a big conglomerate. (타)

두 회사가 합병되어 큰 대기업이 되었다.

Andy Martin ltd. is going to merge with Jason Chemicals Inc. next upcoming January to be a conglomerate.

앤디 마틴 주식회사는 제이슨 화학 회사와 다음 번 다가오는 1월에 대기업이 되기 위해 합병할 예정이다.

002. Before we take care of the final bidding, we should double check _____ numbers and numerical analysis.

   (A) ourselves
   (B) ours
   (C) our
   (D) us

정답) C

해설) bidding 입찰   take care of 처리하다   double check 재확인하다

numerical analysis 수치 해석 (numerical은 number의 형용사임)

주어가 we이므로 빈칸에 소유격 our가 명사 대신 들어갈 수 있음.

Before we take care of the final bidding, we should double check our numbers and numerical analysis.

최종 입찰을 처리하기 전에 우리는 우리의 숫자와 수치 해석을 재확인해야 한다.

003. The Metropolitan arts exhibition consists of _____ paintings and artifacts by many municipal artists and residents.

    (A) when
    (B) or
    (C) if
    (D) both

정답) D

해설) Metropolitan 대도시의 arts exhibition 예술 전시
consist of~ ~으로 구성되다 artifacts 예술작품
municipal 시의 residents 거주민
의미상으로 Both A and B A와 B 둘 다가 적절함.
The Metropolitan arts exhibition consists of both paintings and artifacts by many municipal artists and residents.
대도시 예술 전시는 많은 시의 예술가와 거주민들에 의한 회화와 예술품으로 구성되어 있다.

004. A _____ version of Mr. Markerson's book will be sent to the chief editor for the next month publication.

    (A) revise
    (B) revised
    (C) revising
    (D) revision

정답) B

해설) 문맥상 정답은 revised version임. be sent to~ ~에게 전해지다
chief editor 편집장 publication 출판

005. Be sure to _____ the notice which contains essential information concerning reshuffle of personnel to every employee.

(A) distribute
(B) distributed
(C) to distribute
(D) to be distributed

정답) A

해설) Be sure to~ 반드시 ~하다 / to 다음에 동사원형이 와야 함.

notice 통지서 contain 담고 있다 essential information 필수 정보

concerning = regarding = with regard to ~에 관하여

reshuffle of personnel 인사이동

006. Maxim and Maxima International Champions attracted a _____ of 200 guests with paid admission for the performance.

(A) goal
(B) total
(C) final
(D) purpose

정답) B

해설) 의미상 정답은 total임. attract 유치하다

a total of~ ~의 총합 guests with paid admission 유료 입장 손님

어휘 실력 기르기 02

007. The number of visitors to Jason & Jamie Cosmetics' web site has tripled _____ a year.

(A) within
(B) out of
(C) at
(D) then

정답) **A**

해설) The number of~ ~의 숫자   has tripled 세 배가 되다   triple 세 배, 세 배가 되다
의미상 within a year가 정답임.   with a year 1년 이내에

008. When listing _____ on your application, you should refer to exact titles and specific dates.

(A) accomplishing
(B) accomplished
(C) accomplishments
(D) accomplish

정답) **C**

해설) list A on B B에 A를 기입하다, 목록으로 적다   refer to 언급하다, 참조하다
exact titles 정확한 제목   specific dates 구체적인 날짜

009. During the promotional _____ the customers who pay a visit to Macy's department store in New York can get more discount rate.

(A) shop
(B) period
(C) part
(D) authority

정답) **B**

해설) 정답은 period임.   During the promotional period 판촉 기간 동안에
pay a visit to~ ~를 방문하다   get more discount rate 할인율을 더 받다

010. After continuous trial and error Nelson Independent Chemicals has floated _____ its company on the stock market.

(A) successful
(B) successively
(C) successfully
(D) succession

정답) C

해설) After continuous trial and error 끊임없는 시행착오 후에

float its company on the stock market 주식시장에 회사를 상장하다

문장의 구조가 완전하므로 의미 적절한 부사가 들어감.

정답은 successfully임.   successfully 성공적으로   successively 연속적으로

의미상 성공적으로 회사를 상장했다는 맥락이므로 successfully를 골라야 함.

011. With newly launched mobile phones gaining popularity, you will find _____ for sale at many off line stores as well as online.

(A) they
(B) their
(C) them
(D) themselves

정답) C

해설) 앞에 나온 명사 mobile phones를 지칭하므로 정답은 대명사 them이다.

off line stores as well as online 온라인뿐만 아니라 오프라인 상점에서도

With newly launched mobile phones gaining popularity

새로 출시한 휴대폰이 인기를 얻고 있는 가운데

012. Motorists are _____ recommended to drive with much care especially at night on the wet roads.

(A) strongly
(B) strength

(C) strong

(D) stronger

정답) A

해설) be recommended to 이하가 완전한 문장을 갖추고 있으므로 빈칸에는 부사가 들어감.

be recommended to~ ~하도록 추천되다   with much care = very carefully

on the wet roads 젖은 도로에서

어휘 실력 기르기 03

013. The Canadian prime minister, John Mcguill raised more _____ two million dollars for environmental protection and reducing co2 gas.

(A) than

(B) as

(C) even

(D) over

정답) A

해설) 비교급＋than이다. 정답은 A이다.

more than two million dollars 2백만 달러 이상   prime minister 총리

for environmental protection and reducing co2 gas 환경보호와 이산화탄소 감축을 위해

014. Maria and Marion Enterprise Inc. specialize in military database by _____ solutions and security in case of hacking.

(A) provide

(B) provides

(C) provided

(D) providing

정답) D

해설) specialize in~ ~을 전문으로 하다   by 다음에는 동명사가 나와야 함.

by providing solutions and security in case of hacking

해킹이 발생하는 경우에 해결책과 보안을 제공하면서

015. Despite several times of distribution of information, many employees were _____ of operating security system.

(A) willing

(B) sensitive

(C) unaware

(D) undesirable

정답) C

해설) willing 기꺼이 하는   sensitive 민감한   unaware 알지 못하는

undesirable 바람직하는 않은

Despite several times of distribution of information 대여섯 번의 정보 배포에도 불구하고

의미상 be unaware of가 적절함. 정답은 unaware임.

016. All forms of payment _____ cyber money can be accepted and circulated on the game web site, DigiMon.

(A) at

(B) toward

(C) of

(D) including

정답) D

해설) All forms of payment 모든 형태의 지불   cyber money 인터넷 상의 돈

be accepted and circulated 수용되고 유통된다

문맥상 정답은 including임.

017. The _____ features of LX 12 mobile phone are its unique information security and speedy process of text messages.

    (A) distinctly

    (B) distinctive

    (C) distinction

    (D) distinctively

정답) B

해설) 빈칸 다음에 명사가 나오므로 의미 적절한 형용사가 들어감. 정답은 distinctive임.

    distinctive 독특한, 차별적인, 두드러진   unique 독특한

    speedy process of text messages 문자에 대한 빠른 처리

018. Most of the critics in the modern arts officially _____ that Angela's some paintings are forgery by the European Arts Appraisal Association.

    (A) promote

    (B) cite

    (C) craft

    (D) argue

정답) D

해설) 정답은 argue임. 뒤에 that이 나오기 때문에 호응관계를 이룸.

    officially argue that~ 공식적으로 that 이하에 대해 논쟁을 벌이다

    forgery 위작, 조작된 작품

어휘 실력 기르기 04

019. Jason McMillan officially heard that she got _____ time to submit her application for the job opening in search of an accountant.

(A) about
(B) next
(C) still
(D) ever

정답) C

해설) 정답은 still임.   she got still time to~ 여전히 ~할 시간이 있다.

submit her application 그녀의 응시원서를 제출하다

for the job opening in search of an accountant 회계사를 찾는 (일의) 빈자리를 위해

020. Of all the applicants seeking the job of accountant, Mr. Giambee is viewed as the

_____.

(A) qualification
(B) most qualified
(C) qualified
(C) more qualified

정답) B

해설) 정답은 the most qualified임. of와 같은 한정 표현이 올 때 the + 최상급을 쓸 수 있음.
Of all the applicants seeking the job of accountant 회계사 일을 찾는 모든 지원자들 중에서
the most qualified 가장 자격을 잘 갖춘

021. _____ your annual donations are not overdue, you are supposed to take all the
rights as a patron of Pederson Foundations.

(A) But
(B) In case of
(C) As long as
(D) Rather than

정답) C

해설) 의미상 해마다 내는 기부가 늦어지지 않는다면 이라는 조건의 맥락을 위 문장이 가지고
있으므로 정답은 As long as임. In case of는 전치사구로서 뒤에 명사(구)가 올 때 씀.

As long as your annual donations are not overdue, you are supposed to take all the rights as a patron of Pederson Foundations.

당신의 해마다 하는 기부의 기일이 늦어지지 않는다면, 페더슨 재단의 후원자로서 모든 권리를 가지도록 되어 있다.

022. The breathtaking mountainous view is the _____ many tourists come to Switzerland all the year round.

(A) reasonable
(B) reasoning
(C) reasoned
(D) reason

정답) D

해설) breathtaking 숨 막히는   mountainous 산으로 둘러싸인, 산맥의
all the year round 1년 내내
문맥에서 빈칸 다음에 뒤의 문장이 완전한 형태이므로 정답은 the reason why이며 why 는 생략이 가능하여 the reason이 됨.

023. The prime minister contributed significantly to _____ his country as the superpower in Europe.

(A) rebuilds
(B) rebuilding
(C) rebuilt
(D) being rebuilt

정답) B

해설) contribute to~ ~에 기여하다   to가 전치사이므로 동명사가 뒤따름.
prime minister 수상   superpower 강대국

024. Mark Pierson Inc. offers a wide range of _____ quality display gadgets in the country.

(A) afford

(B) affordable

(C) affording

(D) affords

정답) B

해설) affordable ~유지할 만한, 가격이 알맞은   a wide range of~ 광범위한

quality display gadgets 품질 좋은 디스플레이 장치

어휘 실력 기르기 05

025. Martin Kensington, _____ marketing strategy, is very effective to the target customers, is going to deliver a keynote speech at the conference.

(A) whom

(B) what

(C) which

(D) whose

정답) D

해설) Martin Kensington과 뒤에 나오는 marketing strategy가 일종의 소유 관계를 이루므로 관계 대명사 소유격을 씀.

target customers 목표 고객   deliver a keynote speech 기조연설을 하다

026. Miller Klarkson _____ the direction of famous legend singer Michael Kimberly will be performing a live concert tonight.

(A) to

(B) under

(C) around

(D) at

정답) B

해설) 주어인 Miller Klarkson 다음에 Miller Klarkson을 수식하는 전치사구가 필요하며 문맥의 의미상 under가 정답임.

under the direction of~ ~의 지도하에   perform a concert 콘서트를 공연하다

027. Promoting sales and inviting customers from New York _____ due to severe rainfalls and unstable weather.

(A) postponed
(B) is postponing
(C) will postpone
(D) was postponed

정답) D

해설) 위 선택 사항에서 정답은 was postponed임. postpone은 타동사로 연기하다임.

postpone = delay = put off 연기하다, 미루다

due to = owing to = thanks to ~때문에

severe rainfalls and unstable weather 심한 비와 불안정한 날씨

028. After _____ investment in production capacity, Miller Brewers has increased its revenue by 20 percent.

(A) substantial
(B) substance
(C) substantially
(D) substantiate

정답) A

해설) 의미상 생산 용량의 실제적인 증가 후에 밀러 브루어스(주류회사)가 수입을 20퍼센트까지 증가시켰다는 의미이므로 빈칸에는 substantial이 적절함.

substantial 실제적인   substantial investment 실제적인 투자

substantiate 실증하다, 입증하다   increase revenue 수입을 증가시키다

029. You should _____ to the changes not to have any damage on your computer network.

(A) promote
(B) undo
(C) revert
(D) boot

정답) C

해설) promote 촉진하다, 승진하다   undo 실행하지 않다 (타동사)

revert 되돌리다, 되돌아가다 (to 전치사 동반함)   boot (컴퓨터) 시동을 켜다

문맥상 to라는 전치사가 동반되므로 revert가 정답임.

You should revert to the changes not to have any damage on your computer process.

컴퓨터 네트워크에 피해를 입지 않으려면 변경을 되돌려야 한다.

030. *Time* magazine as well as *Newsweek* will go through _____ transformation from print to electronic.

(A) publication
(B) undecided
(C) representation
(D) contribution

정답) A

해설) 정답은 publication임. 문맥상 출판 변화를 겪는다는 뜻임.

B as well as A = Not only A but also B A뿐만 아니라 B도

go through 겪다, 경험하다   go through publication transformation 출판 변화를 겪다

from print to electronic 인쇄에서 전자상으로

031. The _____ atmosphere of Kommpson co. promotes more productivity in spite of tension between workers.

   (A) competitiveness
   (B) compete
   (C) competitive
   (D) competitor

정답) C

해설) 문맥상 명사 앞의 빈칸이므로 의미 적절한 형용사가 와야 한다. 정답은 competitive임.

competitive 경쟁의, 경쟁력 있는   competitiveness 경쟁력

compete 경쟁하다   competitor 경쟁자

The competitive atmosphere of Kommpson co. promotes more productivity in spite of tension between workers.

콤슨 회사의 경쟁하는 분위기는 노동자들 사이에서 긴장을 일으킴에도 불구하고 더 많은 생산성을 촉진한다.

032. Thanks to his _____ for the revival of industrial city, Malcome Jackson was able to run for mayor election.

   (A) patronizing
   (B) patronizes
   (C) patronage
   (D) patronized

정답) C

해설) 소유격 다음에 명사이므로 정답은 patronage임.   patronize 후원하다   patronage 후원

Thanks to~ = Because of = On account of ~때문에

run for mayor election 시장 선거에 출마하다

033. Security system is the top _____ in the cyber space and internet environment in the world.

(A) privacy
(B) priority
(C) premium
(D) product

정답) B

해설) 정답은 top priority임.   top priority 최우선 순위

security system 안전 시스템   internet environment 인터넷 환경

034. New employee training program was composed of teaching and practice by much _____ staff members.

(A) experienced
(B) experience
(C) experiencing
(D) experiences

정답) A

해설) 정답은 experienced. 많은 경험이 있는 직원들이라는 의미이므로 수동태 표현이 와야 함.

be composed of~ = consist of ~으로 구성되다

035. It was the third _____ month of sales increases, while production had its biggest rise in 15 months.

(A) being consecutive
(B) consecutive
(C) consecutively
(D) being consecutively

정답) B

해설) 정답은 consecutive임. 의미 적절한 형용사가 동반되어야 함.

sales increase 매출 증가

036. The company will sharply _____ production of A 12, its most expensive smart phone as demand on premium mobile phones dwindles.

(A) curtail
(B) cutting
(C) cuts
(D) curtails

정답) A

해설) 조동사 will 다음에 빈칸이 나왔으므로 동사원형을 써야 하며 의미상 줄인다는 의미이므로 cut 혹은 curtail이 되어야 함.

curtail = cut back 삭감하다   dwindle = decrease 줄다, 줄어들다

The company will sharply curtail production of A 12, its most expensive smart phone as demand on premium mobile phones dwindles.

회사는 프리미엄 모바일 폰의 수요가 줄어듦에 따라 가장 값비싼 스마트폰인 A12의 생산을 급격히 줄일 것이다.

어휘 실력 기르기 07

037. Meridian Hamilton Inc. would need to significantly _____ its production and shave operating costs due to economic slowdown.

(A) streamline
(B) start
(C) strike
(D) stick

정답) A

해설) 정답은 streamline임. 문맥상 생산을 효율화하고 운영비를 줄인다는 의미이므로 선택 사항 중에서 streamline이 가장 적절함.   streamline 간소화 하다

shave operating costs 운영비를 절감하다   due to economic slowdown 경기 침체 때문에

038. The company _____ its centennial on Thursday with plans to sharpen its focus on innovation and ambitious enterprises for supersonic commercial flight.

(A) marking
(B) marked
(C) marker
(D) to mark

정답) B

해설) 정답은 marked임. 전체 문장의 동사가 없으므로 동사가 필요함.

mark centennial 백 주년을 기념하다

sharpen its focus on innovation 혁신의 초점을 분명히 하다

ambitious enterprises 야심찬 계획   for supersonic commercial flight 초음속 여객기

039. Mr. Markerson all the time _____ to recognize and admire the individual achievements of his team members in the company.

(A) talks
(B) thinks
(C) strives
(D) focuses

정답) C

해설) 정답은 strive임.   strive to~ ~하려고 노력하다

talk to~ ~에게 말하다 (to는 전치사로서 뒤에 사람이 옴)

focus on~ ~에 초점을 맞추다   all the time = always 항상

recognize and admire 인정하고 칭찬하다 (둘 다 타동사이므로 뒤에 목적어가 나옴)

040. _____ purchase of Airbus A380 with the largest seating capacity, the final decision from the board of directors should be made.

(A) By
(B) Prior to
(C) Since
(D) Into

정답) B

해설) 정답은 prior to임. ~하기 전에   the final decision 최종 결정
be made 이루어지다   the board of directors 이사회
with the largest seating capacity 가장 많은 좌석 용량을 가진
Prior to purchase of Airbus A380 with the largest seating capacity, the final decision
from the board of directors should be made.
가장 많은 좌석 용량을 가진 에어버스 A380을 구매하기 전에 이사회의 최종 결정이 이루
어져야 한다.

041. Kempton International Catering announces that the company will release _____
brand new salad dishes this year.

(A) custom
(B) customized
(C) customs
(D) custom

정답) B

해설) 정답은 customized임. 문맥상 맞춤형 새로운 메뉴를 출시한다는 의미이며 빈칸에 형용사
형태가 들어가야 함.
release 출시하다   customize 고객의 요구에 맞추다   custom 관습   customs 세관

042. Melany Kahill was _____ as the journalist of the year with the article on the
upcoming mayor election.

(A) naming
(B) names
(C) named
(D) name

정답) C

해설) 정답은 named임.   be named as~ ~로 명명되다
as the journalist of the year 올해의 언론인으로
with the article on the upcoming mayor election 다가오는 시장 선거에 관한 기사로

043. You'd better upgrade your contactable information _____ submitting your application for the job opening.

    (A) to
    (B) before
    (C) at
    (D) within

정답) B

해설) 정답은 before임. 문맥상 취업 지원서를 제출한 후에 연락 가능한 정보를 업그레이드 하라는 의미이므로 before가 적절함.　had better + 동사원형~ ~하는 게 더 낫다
before submitting your application for the job opening 취업 지원서를 제출하기 전에

044. Amid increasing _____, the IT company made a lot of efforts to develop innovative items.

    (A) competition
    (B) competitive
    (C) competitiveness
    (D) compete

정답) A

해설) 정답은 competition임. 문맥상 경쟁이 치열한 가운데 라는 의미이므로 competition이 적절함. competition 경쟁　competitive 경쟁력 있는　competitiveness 경쟁력　compete 경쟁하다
made a lot of efforts to develop innovative items
혁신적인 품목을 개발하려고 많은 노력을 기울였다

045. All _____ will take place at Grand Multipurpose Stage in the heart of New York City.

(A) perform

(B) performer

(C) performs

(D) performances

정답) D

해설) 정답은 performances임. 문맥상 주어 자리이므로 명사가 올 수 있는데 performer는 공연하는 사람이고 performances는 공연이다. take place 발생하다, 일어나다 라는 동사가 뒤따르므로 주어는 performances가 적절함. in the heart of~ ~의 중심부에

046. The repairman will _____ a close inspection of any defected parts in the production line.

(A) look

(B) repair

(C) conduct

(D) search

정답) C

해설) 정답은 conduct임. conduct a close inspection 면밀한 검사를 수행하다
look ~처럼 보이다 search는 뒤에 전치사 for가 와야 함. search for = find
a close inspection of any defected parts in the production line
생산 라인의 결함 있는 부품에 대한 면밀한 검사

047. Top Celestial Inc. tries to employ _____ staff and to promote potentials of the workers.

(A) diversify

(B) diversely

(C) diversity

(D) diverse

정답) D

해설) 정답은 diverse임. 빈칸 다음에 명사가 나오므로 형용사가 적절함.

diversify 다양화 하다   diverse 다양한   diversity 다양성   diversely 다양하게
to promote potentials of the workers 직원의 잠재력을 촉진하기 위해

048. Matt Motors is _____ to developing electric cars for the purpose of pursuing harmless and clean fuel of the car.

(A) committed
(B) commits
(C) committing
(D) commit

정답) A

해설) 정답은 committed임.   be committed to~ ~하는 데 헌신하다 (to는 전치사임)

for the purpose of~ ~의 목적을 위해

pursuing harmless and clean fuel of the car 무해하고 깨끗한 자동차 연료를 추구함

어휘 실력 기르기 09

049. Mark Jacob volunteered to give a hand to the department of customer service _____ he had never worked for the department.

(A) despite
(B) in spite
(C) although
(D) even

정답) C

해설) 정답은 although임. 빈칸 뒤에 문장이 뒤따르므로 접속사가 와야 함. 선택지에서 접속사는 although만 가능함.   despite = in spite of 전치사이고, even은 부사임.

give a hand to~ ~를 돕다   volunteer to~ ~하기 위해 자원하다

050. _____ the fact that Taster's Coffee Brewers are available online, most of the customers purchase them from the stores.

(A) Though
(B) Even though
(C) In spite
(D) Despite

정답) D

해설) 정답은 despite임. the fact라는 명사가 빈칸 다음에 나오므로 전치사가 들어가야 함.

despite = in spite of ~에도 불구하고 (전치사)

even though = though = although는 접속사이므로 뒤에 주어와 동사가 나와야 함.

despite the fact that~ that 이하의 사실에도 불구하고

051. From candles to jewelry, Melike's Boutique has the perfect gift for any _____.

(A) occasioned
(B) occasional
(C) occasion
(D) occasionally

정답) C

해설) 정답은 occasion임. 어떠한 경우라도 적합한 선물이 준비되어 있다는 의미를 내포하고 있음.

occasion 경우, 행사   occasional 가끔의   occasionally 가끔씩

052. Dr. Cabot intends to replace the furniture in the meeting room to make it more _____ for patients.

(A) comfortable
(B) reachable
(C) probable
(D) capable

정답) A

해설) 정답은 comfortable임. 환자에게 편안하게 해준다는 문맥이 적절함.

to make it more comfortable for patients 환자를 위해 더 편안한 방을 만들기 위해서

053. Because the CEO's statements were not quoted _____, the interview must be revised before the publication.

(A) corrects
(B) correctly
(C) correcting
(D) correction

정답) B

해설) 정답은 correctly임. 위 문장에서 사장의 언급이 정확하게 인용되지 않았다는 맥락이므로 correctly가 적절함. must be revised 수정되어야만 한다 before publication 출판 전에

054. The building contractors offered the Kelstham Electrical the same contract terms _____ were offered to them last year.

(A) whose
(B) when
(C) that
(D) they

정답) C

해설) 정답은 that임. the same contract terms 똑같은 계약 조건

빈칸 이후에 주어가 빠져 있으므로 불완전한 문장이다. 불완전한 문자에서 관계대명사가 쓰인다. terms는 관계 대명사 which나 that을 쓸 수 있다.

055. The author revealed that the ideas from her novels were drawn _____ from her experiences growing up in Spain.

(A) ideally
(B) largely
(C) seemingly
(D) probably

정답) B

해설) 정답은 largely임. 의미적절한 부사로는 largely가 알맞다.

be drawn from~ ~로부터 도출되다   be drawn largely from~ ~로부터 대부분 도출되다

056. The events committee _____ requested that Cherman's Caterers provide the food for this year's holiday party.

(A) specifics
(B) specified
(C) specifically
(D) specified

정답) C

해설) 정답은 specifically임. 문장의 구조가 완전하므로 더 이상 부족한 요소가 없다. 이럴 때 부사가 들어간다. request와 같은 명령, 요구, 제안의 동사 다음에는 that 절에서 should가 생략되어 동사원형이 오는 것에 주의해야 함.

specifically requested 구체적으로 요청했다

057. Ms. Wordington _____ the keynote speech at the Vision in Ecotourism convention.

(A) delivered
(B) achieved
(C) pursued

(D) implied

정답) A

해설) 정답은 delivered임.　delivered the keynote speech 기조연설을 했다

give a speech = deliver a speech 연설하다

058. Same-day-delivery can be scheduled _____ you place your order before 10 A.M.

(A) if
(B) for
(C) yet
(D) either

정답) A

해설) 정답은 if임. 빈칸 다음에 주어와 동사가 들어간 문장이 나오고 있으므로 접속사가 필요하며 선택지에서 if가 가능함.

Same-day-delivery 당일 배송　place an order = make an order 주문하다

059. The Gregston Hotel's flexibility regarding check-in time is an _____ of its commitment to customer satisfaction.

(A) indicating
(B) indicative
(C) indication
(D) identified

정답) B

해설) 정답은 indication임. 관사 다음에 명사가 와야 하며 선택지에서 indication만 명사임.

indication 지시, 표시　indicate 지시하다, 가리키다

060. Some seats are still available in the third row for the people who want a closer _____ of the stage.

(A) view

(B) sight

(C) watch

(D) show

정답) A

해설) 정답은 view임. 비슷한 의미의 어휘이지만 관객의 입장에서는 view를 보는 것이므로 view를 씀. I have a clear view of the stage 나는 무대가 잘 보인다

어휘 실력 기르기 11

061. Players around the world are in search of rare and valuable game items and connect _____ each other.

(A) once

(B) then

(C) with

(D) just

정답) C

해설) 정답은 with임. connect with~ ~와 연결하다 rare 드문 valuable 귀중한
be in search of = search for 찾다 connect with each other 서로 연결하다

062. The municipal chief director in transportation said that the _____ challenge is that the city should construct subway stations.

(A) significance

(B) signifier

(C) significantly

(D) most significant

정답) D
해설) 정답은 most significant임.   the most significant challenge 가장 의미 있는 도전

the municipal chief director in transportation 시 교통 수석 국장

063. _____ waste of fossil fuel during production has caused air pollution and the health problem among the staffs.

   (A) Sure
   (B) A lot
   (C) Many
   (D) Excessive

정답) D

해설) 정답은 excessive임. 문맥상 waste라는 명사를 꾸미는 의미 적절한 형용사가 필요함.

a lot of~ ~이면 쓸 수 있음.   excessive 지나친

Excessive waste of fossil fuel during production has caused air pollution and the health problem among the staffs.

생산하는 동안에 화석 연료의 지나친 소모가 대기 오염과 직원의 건강 문제를 야기했다.

064. Peli and Keli clothing store is very fashionable and popular among customers because it is attractive and _____ priced.

   (A) affordably
   (B) affordability
   (C) affording
   (D) affords

정답) A

해설) 정답은 affordably임.   fashionable 패셔너블한, 패션 감각이 있는

it is attractive and affordably priced. 매력적이고 가격이 적당하다.

be priced 가격이 형성되다   It is low priced 가격이 싸다

It is high priced 가격이 비싸다

065. Manhattan General Hospital is reliable, since it employs the _____ doctors from the many medical fields.

(A) qualification
(B) qualifies
(C) quality
(D) qualified

정답) D

해설) 정답은 qualified임.   doctors라는 명사를 수식하는 의미 적절한 형용사가 필요함.

reliable 믿을 만한   qualified doctors 자격 있는 의사들

qualify 자격을 부여하다   quality 자격

066. Neither the price _____ the quality of the smart phone GK15 is satisfying mobile phone users.

(A) with
(B) nor
(C) or
(D) though

정답) B

해설) 정답은 nor임.   neither A nor B A도 B도 ～이 아니다

Neither the price nor the quality of the smart phone GK15 is satisfying mobile phone users. GK15 스마트폰의 가격도 품질도 휴대폰 사용자들을 만족시키지 않는다.

어휘 실력 기르기 12

067. Due to _____ layoff large number of employees in the sales department left the company.

(A) invalid

(B) massive

(C) void

(D) vacant

정답) B

해설) 의미상으로 대량 해고 때문이므로 massive가 정답임.

Due to massive layoff large number of employees in the sales department left the company. 대량 해고 때문에 영업부의 많은 직원들이 회사를 떠났다.

invalid 유효하지 않은   void 공허한   vacant 텅 빈

068. Be sure to bring your _____ receipts when requesting reimbursement for travel expenses.

(A) signed

(B) signs

(C) singing

(D) to sign

정답) A

해설) 정답은 signed임. 빈칸 뒤의 receipts라는 명사를 꾸며주므로 의미 적절한 형용사가 필요함.

request reimbursement for travel expenses 여행 경비 상환을 요청하다

Be sure to~ 반드시 ~하다

069. Law _____ on illegally imported building materials was announced in order to prevent any smuggler.

(A) supplies

(B) recruitment

(C) enforcement

(D) authorities

정답) C

해설) 정답은 enforcement임. law enforcement 법률 집행   law enforcement official 경관
supplies 공급   recruitment 구직   illegally imported 불법으로 수입된   smuggler 밀수업자

070. _____ the CEO, the managing director announced that the company is going to merge with another IT company.

(A) Provided that
(B) Because
(C) Between
(D) On behalf of

정답) D
해설) 정답은 on behalf of임.   on behalf of~ ~을 대신하여
managing director 전무이사   merge with 합병하다
provided that = providing that = if = in case that (접속사임)

071. By means of shaving the costs, the company is heavily depending _____ the assistance from the volunteers around the world.

(A) among
(B) on
(C) up
(D) into

정답) B
해설) 정답은 on임.   depend on = rely on = count on 의지하다
by means of~ ~의 방법으로   shave the costs 비용을 절감하다
the assistance from the volunteers around the world 전 세계 자원봉사자들의 원조

072. Even though other seats in the airplane remain empty during the flight you should not _____ them.

(A) occupancy

(B) approach

(C) occupy

(D) approaching

정답) C

해설) 정답은 occupy임.　occupy 점유하다, 차지하다　occupancy 점유　approach 접근하다

비행기에서는 지정 좌석에만 앉아야 하므로 다른 좌석이 비었다고 그 좌석을 차지해서는

안 되므로 문맥상 occupy가 적절함.

어휘 실력 기르기 13

073. For the purpose of security _____ at the production line, all the workers should wear identification badges.

(A) being enhanced

(B) to enhance

(C) enhancement

(D) enhanced

정답) C

해설) 정답은 enhancement임.

for the purpose of security enhancement 보안 증진의 목적을 위해

wear identification badges 신분증 배지를 착용하다

074. The MTV provides full _____ of Academy Awards in 2016 at Channel 25 tonight.

(A) coverage

(B) curtailing

(C) cut

(D) cushion

정답) **A**

해설) 정답은 coverage임.   coverage는 보도, 방송의 의미임. (보험의 보장범위도 있음)
provide 제공하다   curtailing 삭감

075. _____ Mr. Markerson tried to play the augmented-reality game like Pokemon Go,
he could not enjoy it well due to connection delay.

(A) Despite
(B) Eventually
(C) In spite
(D) Even though

정답) **D**

해설) 정답은 even though임. 빈칸 뒤에 문장이 나오므로 의미 적절한 접속사를 골라야 함.
the augmented-reality game like Pokemon Go 포켓몬 고와 같은 증강현실 게임
due to connection delay 접속 지체로 인해

076. Today a featured speaker on auto industry will _____ cyber security in mobile
phones.

(A) address
(B) talk
(C) envelop
(D) inspect

정답) **A**

해설) 정답은 address임. 주어가 a featured speaker(초청 연사)이므로 address(연설하다)가 적절함.
talk about(~에 대해 말하다)이나 talk to(~에게 말하다)가 되어야 함.
inspect 검사하다   envelop 봉투, 감싸다 (동사)

077. Among the contenders for the best actor Mr. Parker _____ the prize of Actor of
the Year.

(A) awarding

(B) was awarded

(C) awarded

(D) having awarded

정답) B

해설) 정답은 was awarded임.   contender 경쟁자   among the contenders 경쟁자들 사이에서
be awarded 수상하다   the prize of Actor of the Year 올해의 배우상

078. Despite the spirited discussion concerning increase in overtime payment, the management could not _____ it.

(A) finalize

(B) deal

(C) tell

(D) talk to

정답) A

해설) 정답은 finalize임.   finalize 마무리 짓다 (타동사)   deal with~ ~을 다루다 (with 동반)
tell somebody something ~에게 ...을 말하다 (수여동사 형태임)
talk to~ ~에게 말하다   the management 경영진
Despite the spirited discussion 열띤 논쟁에도 불구하고
concerning increase in overtime payment 초과수당 인상에 관하여

어휘 실력 기르기 14

079. The foreign company, Nintendo nowadays _____ in a video game which makes use of augmented-reality.

(A) specialists
(B) specialty
(C) specializes
(D) specializing

정답) C
해설) 정답은 specialize임. 전체 문장의 동사가 필요하므로 specialize가 적절함.

specialize in~ ~을 특화하다   augmented-reality 증강현실   make use of~ ~을 이용하다

080. Many analysts in Europe will consider how banks are _____ the so-called Brexit vote.

(A) responded
(B) responds
(C) respondent
(D) responding to

정답) D
해설) 빈칸에 적절한 답은 be respondent to나 be responding to 둘 중 하나이다.

be respondent to~ ~에 반응하다   be responding to~ ~에 반응하고 있는 중이다 (진행)

Brexit는 Britain + Exit의 합성어로 영국이 Euro 탈퇴여부를 결정짓기 위해 했던 국민투표의 별칭을 말함.

081. You'd better be _____ that the smart phone you ordered from our online web site is no longer available.

(A) advise
(B) advice
(C) advised
(D) advises

정답) C
해설) 정답은 advised임. be 동사 다음에 수동태가 되어야 함.

be advised that~ that 이하에 대해서 조언을 듣다

no longer available 더 이상 이용가능하지 않다

082. Employees should _____ not to use the main photocopier at the supply room until the machine is fixed.

(A) be parted
(B) be informed
(C) be attended
(D) be respected

정답) B

해설) 정답은 be informed임.   be informed not to use~ 사용하지 않도록 정보를 전달받다
photocopier 복사기   supply room 보급실

083. Manfred Peterson serves as a courier service manager in New York branch for _____ years without a break.

(A) conducting
(B) confined
(C) consecutive
(D) conformed

정답) C

해설) 정답은 consecutive임. 뒤에 나온 명사를 수식해야 하므로 형용사가 되어야 하며 의미상 consecutive가 적절함.
consecutive 연속적인   conducting 수행하는   confined 제한된
conformed 따르는   without a break 쉬지 않고
serve as a courier service manager 택배업체 매니저로 일하다

084. At the end of this year our CEO will _____ special training course for the newly employed staffs.

(A) introduced

(B) introduce

(C) introductory

(D) introductions

정답) B

해설) 정답은 introduce임. 조동사 다음에 동사원형이 나옴.

introduce special training course for the newly employed staffs.

새로 고용된 직원들을 위한 특별 훈련 코스를 도입하다.

어휘 실력 기르기 15

085. The _____ file specifies details of the company policy concerning sales enhancement.

(A) attachment

(B) attached

(C) attach

(D) attaching

정답) B

해설) 정답은 attached임. 첨부된 파일이라는 의미이므로 attached file이 알맞음.

attachment 첨부   attach 첨부하다

specifies details of the company policy 회사 정책의 세부사항을 구체화하다

concerning sales enhancement   매출 신장에 관한

086. All the newly employed staffs will receive a/an _____ card to pass the gates and get security.

(A) identification

(B) handbook

(C) partition

(D) parking

정답) A

해설) 정답은 identification임.

의미상 출입할 수 있는 신분증이 있어야 하므로 identification card가 되어야 함.

all the newly employed staffs 새로 고용된 모든 직원들

to pass the gates and get security 문을 출입하고 안전을 확보하기 위해

087. The CEOs of the two companies emphasized that both of them secured _____ the economic partnership.

(A) tradition

(B) traditional

(C) traditionally

(D) traditionalize

정답) C

해설) 정답은 traditionally임. secured 다음에 the economic partnership이라는 목적어가 나오므로 3형식의 완전한 문장이다. 이럴 때 부사가 들어갈 수 있음.

emphasized that~ that 이하를 강조하다

secured traditionally the economic partnership 전통적으로 경제협력을 확보했다

088. The tycoon of the company demanded _____ information regarding how to develop augmented-reality programs from the department of R&D.

(A) details

(B) detailing

(C) detailed

(D) detail

정답) C

해설) 정답은 detailed임. 상세한 정보는 detailed information임.

tycoon 경제계의 거물   information regarding~ ~에 관한 정보

how to develop augmented-reality programs 증강현실 프로그램 개발 방법

the department of R&D 연구 개발 부서

089. The cyber security program has been installed to prevent any _____ hacking and online terrors.

(A) hazardous
(B) lucrative
(C) beneficial
(D) dependent

정답) A

해설) 정답은 hazardous임.

의미상 위험한 해킹을 예방하는 것이므로 부정적인 의미인 hazardous가 적절함.

hazardous 위험한   lucrative 이익이 되는   beneficial 혜택이 되는

dependent 책임 있는   be installed 설치되다

090. The CEO of the company _____ that M&A with Jason Miller Inc. will bring much more benefits in the forseeable future.

(A) scheduled
(B) assured
(C) parted
(D) inserted

정답) A

해설) 정답은 assured임. 의미상 회사의 인수 합병이 혜택을 가져올 것을 확신하는 것이므로 assured를 선택해야 함.

insert 삽입하다   bring much more benefits 더 많은 혜택을 가져오다

in the forseeable future 가까운 미래에

091. The company said that its _____ in the first quarter rose 15 percent due to the countless efforts for sales promotion.

(A) revenue
(B) part
(C) market
(D) schedule

정답) A

해설) 정답은 revenue임. 회사의 수익을 의미함.

in the first quarter 1분기   rose 15 percent 15퍼센트 올랐다

due to the countless efforts for~ ~에 대한 끊임없는 노력 때문에

sales promotion 판매 촉진

092. The _____ scenes of the mountain are famous tourist spot and are attracting many visitors around the world.

(A) remarking
(B) remarkable
(C) remarkably
(D) remark

정답) B

해설) 명사 앞에 빈칸이 있으므로 의미 적절한 형용사가 들어가야 함.

remarkable 눈에 띄는 (형용사)   remarkably 눈에 띄게 (부사)

tourist spot 관광 명소   attract many visitors 많은 방문객들을 끌어들이다

093. _____ the cost estimate, the building renovation is expected to cost another one million dollars.

(A) Aside from
(B) Next to
(C) Instead of
(D) Out of

정답) A

해설) 건물 개축이 비용 견적서 이외에 추가로 백만 달러가 더 들어간다는 의미이므로 빈칸에 aside from이 적절함.

aside from~ ～ 이외에   be expected to~ ～할 것으로 예상되다

cost another one million dollars 추가로 백만 달러의 비용이 들다

094. Thanks to outstanding job performance of the sales team, the company is expected to _____ the contract with the sales manger.

(A) extends
(B) extension
(C) extend
(D) extending

정답) C

해설) 영업 팀의 뛰어난 업무 성과 때문에 회사는 영업부장과 계약을 연장할 것으로 예상된다는 의미이므로 빈칸에 extend가 정답임.

extend the contract 계약을 연장하다

thanks to outstanding job performance 뛰어난 업무 성과 때문에

095. It is predicted that consumer price index will increase _____ 30 and 35 percent compared to last year's.

(A) between
(B) both
(C) either
(D) about

정답) A

해설) 소비자 물가 지수가 작년에 비해 30에서 35 퍼센트 증가한다는 의미이므로 between이
적절함.   between A and B A와 B 사이에
be predicted that~ that 이하가 예상되다   consumer price index 소비자 물가 지수

096. The _____ of governmental development funds is quite crucial, since revenue
and expenditure should be balanced.

(A) allocating
(B) allocate
(C) allocates
(D) allocation

정답) D

해설) 정관가 다음에는 명사가 답임.   allocation 배분   allocate 배분하다
crucial 필수적인, 중요한   governmental development funds 정부 개발 기금
revenue and expenditure should be balanced 수입과 지출이 균형을 이루어야 한다

어휘 실력 기르기 17

097. It is urgently _____ that all the employees should bring their ID cards in order to
enter the office.

(A) require
(B) requires
(C) required
(D) requirement

정답) C

해설) 빈칸에 required가 적절함. quite는 부사로서 의미를 강조함.
It is required that~ that 이하가 필요하다   bring their ID cards 신분증을 가져오다

in order to enter the office 사무실에 들어가기 위해서　urgently 긴급하게

in order to = so as to~ ～하기 위해서 (부정사 부사적 용법임)

098. For your summer leave the department of general affairs demands that you should get _____ from your supervisor in advance.

(A) the sign
(B) the signature
(C) the signing
(D) the signs

정답) B

해설) get이 타동사이므로 뒤에 명사가 나와야 함. 서명을 받다는 뜻은 get the signature임. sign은 표지, 표지판을 의미함. demand that 뒤에 should가 쓰일 수 있고 생략 가능함.

for your summer leave 여름휴가를 위해

the department of general affairs 총무부

from your supervisor in advance 미리 당신의 상사로부터

099. The department of public relations is already trying to _____ an ad of recruitment in the newspaper.

(A) tell
(B) demand
(C) placement
(D) put

정답) D

해설) 광고를 내다 라는 표현은 put an ad = place an ad임.

the department of public relations 홍보부

put an ad of recruitment in the newspaper 신문에 모집 광고를 내다

100. The department of information and security announces that unnecessary data _____ is prohibited especially when you are at the desk.

(A) retrieved

(B) retrieval

(C) retrieving

(D) retrieve

정답) B

해설) 불필요한 데이터 검색은 금지된다는 맥락이므로 정답은 retrieval임.

unnecessary data retrieval 불필요한 데이터 검색

be prohibited 금지되다　be at the desk 책상에 있다 (책상에서 일하다)

101. _____ repeated changes in leadership and strategy Mall & Shoppers Inc. is leading produce circulation in the U.S.

(A) Despite

(B) In spite

(C) Dues

(D) For

정답) A

해설) 의미상으로 리더십과 전략의 반복된 변경에도 불구하고 몰 앤 쇼퍼스는 미국에서 농산물 유통을 이끌고 있다는 맥락이므로 빈칸에 전치사 despite가 적절함.

produce 명사로 쓰일 때는 농산물이라는 뜻임.　produce circulation 농산물 유통

102. The Baby and Johnson ltd. gives the customers refunds only _____ they bring their receipts.

(A) which

(B) how

(C) that

(D) when

정답) D

해설) 의미상으로 when이 들어감.　only when + 주어 + 동사~ ~할 때만

give the customers refunds 고객에게 환불하다

only when they bring their receipts 그들(고객들)이 영수증을 가져올 때만

103. Due to the _____ characteristics of M&A details of it will not be informed to the third parties.

    (A) appropriate
    (B) effective
    (C) careful
    (D) sensitive

정답) D

해설) 빈칸 다음에 명사가 나오므로 빈칸에는 의미 적절한 형용사가 들어가 문맥상 sensitive가 들어감.   Due to ~때문에

Due to the sensitive characteristics of M&A M&A의 민감한 특성 때문에

details of it will not be informed to the third parties

세부 사항이 제3자들에게는 알려지지 않을 것이다

104. Green Plastic Inc. provides customers with fresh fruits from the _____ farms all the year round.

    (A) previous
    (B) local
    (C) region
    (D) exact

정답) B

해설) farms라는 명사를 수식하므로 의미 적절한 형용사 local이 정답임.

    provide A with B   A에게 B를 제공하다   all the year round 1년 내내

105. In spite of _____ reviews, many consumers count on online information on the ratings of restaurants.

(A) compound

(B) fraudulent

(C) magnificent

(D) agile

정답) B

해설) 문맥상 사기성이 있는 긍정적인 리뷰에도 불구하고 많은 소비자들은 레스토랑 순위에 관한 오라인 정보를 의지한다는 의미이므로 빈칸에 fraudulent가 적절함.

fraudulent 사기의   fraud 사기, 거짓   compound 복합적인

magnificent 장엄한   agile 민첩한

106. The recruitment for the job opening will not proceed for a _____ due to complaints by some applicants.

(A) stay

(B) break

(C) session

(D) while

정답) D

해설) 문맥상 잠시 동안 중단된다는 의미이므로 for a while이 적절함.

the recruitment for the job opening 일의 공석을 위한 모집

due to complaints by some applicants 일부 응시자들에 의한 불만 때문에

107. The National Charity Foundation aids children of the disabled _____ subsidizing school tuition.

(A) from

(B) by

(C) to

(D) of

정답) B

해설) the disabled 장애인   subsidize school tuition 학교 수업료를 보조하다

subsidy 보조금   aid = give a hand to = help 지원하다, 돕다

The National Charity Foundation aids children of the disabled by subsidizing school tuition. 국가 자선 재단은 학교 수업료를 보조함으로써 장애인의 아이들을 돕는다.

108. Marilyn Inc. specializes in _____ of identity design of a company to satisfy clients' demand.

(A) create
(B) creates
(C) creatively
(D) creativeness

정답) D

해설) 전치사 다음에는 명사가 나와야 함.   specialize in~ ~을 전문으로 하다
create 창조하다   creative 창조적인   creatively 창조적으로   creativeness 창조성
to satisfy clients' demand 고객의 요구를 만족시키기 위해서
identity design of a company 회사 정체성 디자인

어휘 실력 기르기 19

109. The board of directors approved of remodeling of the hotel to _____ room capacity to satisfy customers' demand.

(A) maximize
(B) specialize
(C) hold
(D) intend

정답) A

해설) 의미상으로 객실 용량을 늘린다는 맥락이므로 정답은 maximize임.

maximize room capacity 객실 용량을 극대화 하다

to satisfy customers' demand 고객의 수요를 충족시키기 위해

the board of directors 이사회

approve of remodeling of the hotel 호텔의 리모델링을 승인하다

110. Supervisors are in _____ of advising their juniors especially when they don't know the direction of the company.

(A) care

(B) charge

(C) chance

(D) change

정답) B

해설) 문맥상 전치사 다음에는 명사가 나오며 의미 적절한 명사는 위 문장에서는 charge임.

be in charge of~ = be responsible for~ ~을 책임지다

supervisor 상사   junior 후임, 후배   especially when~ 특별히 ~할 때

111. The management considers that shaving production costs is a top _____ in times of economic slowdown.

(A) check

(B) pride

(C) priority

(D) crisis

정답) C

해설) 문맥상 경제 하락의 시기에는 생산비용을 절감하는 것이 최우선 순위라는 뜻이므로 정답은 priority임.

the management 경영진   shave production costs 생산비용을 절감하다

in times of economic slowdown 경기하락의 시대에

112. Bulgaria is famous _____ its inexpensive lodging, fantastic seafood, and gorgeous beaches in the Black Sea.

(A) with
(B) for
(C) at
(D) to

정답) B

해설) 문맥상 be famous for임.   be famous for~ ~으로 유명하다

inexpensive lodging 값싼 숙박   gorgeous beaches 멋진 해변   the Black Sea 흑해

113. According to travel magazine _____ travelers try to save money by using cheap flights and lodging.

(A) frugal
(B) economic
(C) lavish
(D) intuitive

정답) A

해설) 문맥상 돈을 아끼는 여행객이므로 frugal이 적절함.   frugal 검소한, 절약하는

economic 경제의   economical 경제적인, 절약하는

lavish 풍부한, 낭비하는   intuitive 직관적인

114. It was true that the company was _____ over 100 years ago, when the present chairman was not born.

(A) sent
(B) established
(C) originated
(D) took place

정답) B

해설) 문맥상 100년 전에 그 회사가 설립된 것이므로 established가 적절함.

It is true that~ that 이하가 사실이다

when the present chairman was not born 현 회장이 태어나지 않았을 때

어휘 실력 기르기 20

115. According to the comments of my _____ Martin Perez is one of the leading consultants in the field of M&A.

(A) adviser
(B) advice
(C) advising
(D) advised

정답) **A**

해설) 문맥상 소유격 다음에는 명사가 나와야 함. 명사는 advice와 adviser인데 논평이라는 표현이 있으므로 adviser가 적절함.

According to the comments of my adviser Martin Perez is one of the leading consultants in the field of M&A. 내 조언자의 논평에 따르면 마틴 페레즈는 M&A 분야에서 최고 컨설턴트 중에 하나이다.

116. The air conditioner of High Tech Development consumes about 50 percent less electricity than _____ products.

(A) reasonable
(B) part
(C) economic
(D) conventional

정답) **D**

해설) 문맥상 conventional이 정답임. 보통 제품 보다 50퍼센트 전기를 덜 쓴다는 뜻이므로
conventional이 들어가야 함.

reasonable 합리적인   economic 경제의   conventional 보편적인

consume about 50 percent less electricity 약 50퍼센트의 적은 전기를 소모하다

117. The sunny hot weather of the region enabled many vineyards to harvest high
_____ grapes for wine this year.

(A) quality
(B) quantity
(C) qualities
(D) quantities

정답) A

해설) 문맥상 quality가 정답임. 고품질의 포도는 high quality grapes임.

enable 목적어 + to부정사: 목적어로 하여금 to 이하 하게 하다

harvest 수확하다   vineyard 포도원, 포도밭

118. Many motorists suffered from ill information, since detour signs were not _____
posted.

(A) adequate
(B) adequately
(C) affluent
(D) affluently

정답) B

해설) 문맥상 adequately가 정답임. be posted는 게시되다 라는 의미의 완전한 문장이므로 의미
적절한 부사가 들어가야 함.

adequate 적절한   adequately 적절하게   affluent 풍부한   affluently 풍부하게

Many motorists suffered from ill information, since detour signs were not adequately
posted. 많은 운전자들은 우회 표지판이 적절하게 게시되지 않아서 잘못된 정보로 인해
고생했다.

119. The executive director responded _____ to assistant manager's business proposal than anyone else.

    (A) being positive

    (B) positively

    (C) more positively

    (D) most positive

정답) C

해설) 문맥상 문장의 구조가 완전하므로 부사가 필요하며 부사 positively가 들어가서 more positively that이 적절함. executive director 상무이사

assistant manager's business proposal 대리의 사업 제안서

120. It is said that the main branch will be renovated next year _____ the approval by the board of directors.

    (A) in case of

    (B) provided that

    (C) in addition to

    (D) as a sign of

정답) A

해설) 문맥상 in case of가 적절함. 주어 동사를 포함하는 문장이 나오면 접속사인 provided that이 쓰이지만 명사구가 나오므로 전치사구가 필요함.

in case of~ ~하는 경우에 (전치사) provided that (접속사)

the approval by the board of directors 이사회의 승인

the main branch will be renovated 본점이 개축될 것이다

121. According to the newspapers many parents wondered at what age they should give their child full _____ to smart phones.

　　(A) access
　　(B) path
　　(C) key
　　(D) route

정답) A

해설) 문맥상 어른들이 아이들에게 스마트폰을 사용하게 하는 내용을 물어 보고 있으므로 정답은 access임.　access 이용, 접근, 사용 (명사), 사용하다 (동사)
path 길　key 열쇠, 핵심　route 길, 도로
give their children full access to smart phones
아이들이 스마트폰의 완전한 이용을 하도록 하다

122. In order to give a hand to charity foundation take a _____ to fill out the survey paper.

　　(A) check
　　(B) part
　　(C) moment
　　(D) look

정답) C

해설) 문맥상 서식을 완성하는 데 잠깐의 짬을 내라는 뜻이므로 정답은 take a moment이며 빈 칸에는 moment가 정답임.
In order to give a hand to~ ~을 돕기 위해서　charity foundation 자선 재단
take a moment to fill out the survey paper 서베이 페이퍼 작성을 위해 짬을 내다

123. For the negotiation of pay increase your last year's signed _____ must be brought with.

(A) contract
(B) contraction
(C) contractor
(D) contracting

정답) A
해설) 문맥상 서명이 된 계약서가 동반되어야 한다는 의미이므로 signed contract가 적절함.
contraction 수축   contractor 계약업체   be brought with 동반되다
for the negotiation of pay increase 임금인상 협상을 위해

124. Common Sense Media polled over 1000 parents in the street found that there was no _____ guideline for children's use of internet.

(A) specification
(B) specify
(C) specifies
(D) specific

정답) D
해설) 문맥상 guideline이라는 명사를 수식하므로 형용사가 필요함.   poll 조사하다
specific 구체적인, 명확한   specify 구체화 하다   specification 상세, 기술
there was no specific guideline 명확한 가이드라인이 없었다
for children's use of internet 아이들의 인터넷 사용에 관하여

125. The _____ guest for the music program received a warm welcome from the audience on the floor.

(A) feature
(B) featured
(C) features
(D) featuring

정답) B

해설) feature 특징 (명사), 특징으로 하다 (동사)   the featured guest 특별 초대 손님
the featured speaker 특별 연사   receive a warm welcome 따뜻한 환대를 받다
from the audience on the floor 현장(플로어)의 청중들로부터

126. The car's financing program and residual value buyback program will reduce the
total costs of _____ the vehicle.

(A) owned
(B) owns
(C) owner
(D) owning

정답) D

해설) 전치사 다음에 빈칸이 있고 그 뒤에 vehicle이라는 명사가 나오므로 vehicle을 목적어로
쓰는 동명사가 적절함.   financing program 금융 프로그램
the total costs of owning the vehicle 차량 소유의 총 비용
residual value buyback program 잔존가치 되사주기 프로그램 (자동차 회사에서 차를 판
후에 잔존가치 만큼 돈을 주고 소비자로부터 차를 다시 사들이는 프로그램)

어휘 실력 기르기 22

127. _____ by the city council members at the municipal conference was
unexpectedly high.

(A) Attendants
(B) Attends
(C) Attendees
(D) Attendance

정답) D

해설) 전체 문장의 동사가 was이므로 주어는 보통 명사의 단수나 추상명사, 물질 명사가 되어야 함. 정답은 Attendance임.　Attendance 출석, 출석률　Attendee 출석자
Attendant 안내인, 수행인　flight attendants 승무원
municipal conference 시 회담　unexpectedly high 예상치 못하게 높은

128. The restaurant was awarded the Clean and Safe Prize due to the servers' regular check to get rid of chemical _____ in vegetables and food supplies.

(A) residues
(B) residing
(C) residence
(D) resign

정답) A

해설) 문맥상 chemical이라는 형용사 다음에 명사가 나와야 하는데 야채와 식자재의 화학 잔존물이라는 의미가 적절하므로 정답은 residues임.
residues 잔존물　reside 살다, 주재하다　residence 거주
resident 거주민　resign 사퇴하다　resignation 사퇴
to get rid of chemical residues in vegetables and food supplies
야채와 식자재의 화학 잔존물들을 제거하기 위해서

129. According to Medical Times many people are _____ of their acid reflux from stomach.

(A) with danger
(B) danger
(C) risk
(D) at risk

정답) D

해설) 정답은 at risk임.　be at risk of~ = be in danger of ~의 위험에 있다
acid reflux from stomach 위장으로부터의 위산 역류
According to Medical Times 의료 타임지에 따르면

130. Jason Markakis had to put his job on _____ due to the late response from his boss yesterday.

(A) hole
(B) hell
(C) hold
(D) home

정답) C

해설) put A on hold A를 보류하다   be put on hold의 수동태 형태로 많이 쓰임.

due to the late response from his boss 사장으로부터의 늦은 반응 때문에

(참고) The proposal should be put on hold 제안이 보류되어야 한다

131. This year's book award recipient, Tabitha Orland, will _____ by her editor, Margo Zeller.

(A) introduce
(B) be introduced
(C) be introducing
(D) have introduced

정답) B

해설) by 이하가 있으므로 수동태 표현이 적합함.

will be introduced by~ by 이하에 의해서 소개될 것이다

This year's book award recipient 올해의 책에 대한 상을 받은 수상자

132. Owing to the high demand for our products, Belwald Footwear shipments may be delayed by _____ days.

(A) several
(B) plentiful
(C) hopeful
(D) other

정답) A

해설) 정답은 several임. be delayed by several days 수일 간 지체되다
owing to high demand 많은 수요 때문에

어휘 실력 기르기 23

133. To be eligible for research grants, applicants must be certified engineers in the country in _____ they reside.

(A) which
(B) where
(C) from
(D) there

정답) A

해설) 정답은 which임. 전치사가 앞에 있으므로 관계부사는 올 수 없음.
in the country in which they reside = in the country where they reside
그들이 거주하는 나라에서

134. Melnar Furnishings allows customers to _____ their bills into five easy monthly payments.

(A) divide
(B) reserve
(C) number
(D) substitute

정답) A

해설) 정답은 divide임. five easy monthly payments 다섯 번의 쉬운 월간 지불
고지서를 다섯 번으로 쉽게 나누어서 낸다는 의미임.

135. We have received an overwhelming _____ to our call for nominees for this year's Employee Award.

(A) responsive
(B) response
(C) responded
(D) respond

정답) B

해설) 정답은 response임.   overwhelming response 압도적인 반응

responsive 반응하는   respond 반응하다

136. Rain can cause a baseball game to be delayed or canceled _____ the field becomes too wet.

(A) or
(B) until
(C) if
(D) and

정답) C

해설) 문맥상 if가 정답임. 야구장이 너무 젖는다면 야구경기의 취소나 연기가 가능하다는 맥락 이므로 가정의 의미를 갖는 if가 적절함.

137. With the rise of online sales, consumers leave home to shop much less _____ than in the past.

(A) frequency
(B) frequent
(C) frequently
(D) frequence

정답) C

해설) 정답은 frequently임. 문장의 구조가 완전하므로 부사가 들어가야 함.

frequently 자주   frequent 빈번한   frequency = frequence 주파수, 빈번함

138. By the end of today's workshop, you will be _____ in using the upgraded software.

(A) legitimate
(B) proficient
(C) practical
(D) official

정답) B

해설) 정답은 proficient임. 연수를 통해 소프트웨어 사용이 능숙해지므로 proficient가 문맥상 적절함. workshop 연수, 수련회 proficient 능숙한

legitimate 합법적인 practical 실제적인, 실용적인

어휘 실력 기르기 24

139. When your application is approved, you will receive your new credit card by mail _____ one week.

(A) once
(B) since
(C) while
(D) within

정답) D

해설) 정답은 within임. 위의 선택사항 중에서 one week와 가장 잘 어울리는 표현은 within이다. within one week = within a week 1주일 이내에

140. It is of little surprise that social, outgoing employees work better _____ teams than alone.

(A) without

(B) in

(C) at

(D) over

정답) B

해설) 정답은 in임.　work better in teams 팀에서 일을 더 잘한다

work better in teams than alone 혼자보다는 팀에서 일을 더 잘한다

141.　The company has tried to increase ＿＿＿＿＿ force by 50 percent in the first quarter for the large revenue this year.

(A) sells

(B) sold

(C) sales

(D) salable

정답) C

해설) 영업 인력이라는 표현은 sales force임.　salable 팔 수 있는 (형용사)

in the first quarter 1사 분기에

for the large revenue this year 올해 많은 수익을 위해

142.　The ＿＿＿＿＿ gear of the car KC12 has vastly increased reported crashes and motorists' injuries.

(A) fault

(B) faulty

(C) faulted

(D) faults

정답) B

해설) 빈칸 다음에 명사가 나오므로 의미 적절한 형용사 faulty가 정답임.

fault 결함　faulty 결함 있는　fault 비난하다, 흠잡다 (동사)

has increased reported crashes 언론에서 보도된 충돌이 늘어나게 했다

143. There were floral _____ in every corner of the street and even in the square for the feast of the city.

(A) excellence
(B) presentation
(C) responsibility
(D) arrangements

정답) C

해설) 꽃꽂이는 floral arrangements임.   for the feast of the city 도시의 축제를 위해
in every corner of the street 거리의 모든 구석에도   even in the square 광장에서도

144. The McMillan Consulting Inc. consults only professional groups _____ the Law Association, and Trusty Management Ltd.

(A) such as
(B) given
(C) because
(D) whether

정답) A

해설) 빈칸 뒤에 명사의 내용이 열거 되고 있으므로 정답은 such as임.
consult only professional groups 전문가 단체에게만 의뢰를 하다

어휘 실력 기르기 25

145. For your cyber security the TS App on your smart phone needs to _____ safety function first.

(A) acknowledge
(B) accomplish

(C) implement

(D) extend

정답) C

해설) implement 이행하다, 실행하다   acknowledge 인정하다   accomplish 이룩하다
extend 확장하다   For your cyber security 사이버 보안을 위해
need to~ ~할 필요가 있다   on your smart phone 당신의 스마트 폰에서
implement safety function first 먼저 안전 기능을 실행하다

146. The duty of the factory manager is to _____ the production of metal parts on a regular basis.

(A) please
(B) resolve
(C) secure
(D) contain

정답) C

해설) to 다음에 동사원형이 나와야 하며 의미상 금속 부품의 생산을 정기적으로 확보한다는
의미의 동사가 필요함.   secure 확보하다   resolve 용해하다, 해결하다
contain 담다, 가두다   please 기쁘게 하다   on a regular basis 규칙적으로

147. Passengers with first-class tickets will _____ a plane first and enjoy quality service in the cabin during the flight.

(A) boards
(B) on board
(C) boarding
(D) board

정답) D

해설) 조동사 다음에 동사원형이 나와야 하므로 board가 정답임.

board the plane 비행기에 탑승하다   on board 탑승하여
(참고) board of directors 이사회   first-class tickets 1등석 티켓
enjoy quality service 질 좋은 서비스를 즐기다

148. The Markerson Millan Corporate's ill _____ produces bad results and soaring complaints from the workers.

(A) managers
(B) manages
(C) management
(D) manage

정답) C

해설) 잘못된 경영이 나쁜 결과와 노동자들부터 치솟는 원망을 사므로 빈칸에는 의미상 management가 정답임.   ill management 잘못된 경영
soaring complaints 치솟는 원망   from the workers 노동자들로부터

149. _____ location of Maritime Hotel is one of its strengths to the guests who frequently use the subway in New York.

(A) Convenient
(B) Convenience
(C) Conveniences
(D) Conveniently

정답) A

해설) 문맥상 형용사 형태인 convenient가 적절함.   convenient location 편리한 위치
one of its strengths 강점 중에 하나이다   to the guests who~ ~하는 손님에게
frequently use~ ~을 자주 이용하다

150. Nowadays electric cars like Tesla are gaining popularity due to _____ of taxes and low maintenance costs.

(A) deducting

(B) deduct

(C) reduction

(D) reduce

정답) C

해설) 세금 감면은 reduction of taxes이고 세금 공제는 deduction of taxes임.

문맥상 reduction이 적절함.   low maintenance costs 낮은 유지비용

Nowadays electric cars like Tesla are gaining popularity

요즘 테슬라 같은 전기차가 인기를 끌고 있다

어휘 실력 기르기 26

151. The total cost of Highway 202 in Mid West will be more expensive, since the company's bid was _____ an estimate.

(A) carefully

(B) merely

(C) modestly

(D) enormously

정답) B

해설) 정답은 merely임.   merely 단순히   modestly 겸손하게

carefully 조심스럽게   enormously 엄청나게

since the company's bid was merely an estimate 회사의 입찰이 단순히 추정치이기 때문에

152. As the _____ company succeeded beyond anyone's guess, the investment of half million turned into close to half a billion.

(A) venture

(B) vent

(C) vend

(D) vending

정답) A

해설) 정답은 venture임. 의미상으로 큰 수익을 낸다는 맥락이므로 venture company임.

As the venture company succeeded beyond anyone's guess

벤처 회사가 사람의 추측을 넘어 성공을 거둠에 따라

the investment of half million turned into close to half a billion

백만 달러 절반의 투자가 10억 달러의 절반에 가깝게 바뀌었다

153. According to newest information source shortly after Poketmon Go was released it became a global _____.

(A) sense

(B) sensation

(C) senses

(D) sensing

정답) B

해설) 정답은 sensation임.   sensation 세상을 놀라게 하는 화재   sense 감각

common sense 상식   shortly after~ ~한 직후에   be released 출시되다

according to newest information source 최신 소식통에 따르면

154. At Global Charming Shampoo Inc, normal shipping is free of charge _____ the distance of delivery.

(A) without

(B) other than

(C) along

(D) regardless of

정답) D

해설) 의미상 정답은 regardless of임. 배달 거리와는 상관없이 보통 선적은 무료라는 뜻임.
normal shipping is free of charge 보통 선적은 무료임.
regardless of the distance of delivery 배달 거리와는 상관없이

155. There are many convenient ways for sightseers to travel New York city _____ walking or driving.

(A) instead
(B) apart
(C) except
(D) rather

정답) C

해설) 정답은 except임.   except = except from = apart from ~을 제외하고
instead of~ ~대신에   sightseer 관광객   convenient ways 편리한 방법
travel 여행 (명사), 여행하다 (동사)

156. The company was at a loss since it was _____ from a real threat to online security from cyber terrorists.

(A) knowing
(B) suffering
(C) seeing
(D) taking

정답) B

해설) 정답은 suffering임. 문맥상 온라인 안전에 대한 실제적인 위협으로 인해 고생한다는 의미가 적절함.   suffer from~ ~로부터 고생하다   online security 온라인 안전
be at a loss = be embarrassed = be perplexed 당황하다

157. In the _____ future the venture capitalist expects to reap enormous revenue from his investment.

    (A) foreseeable
    (B) foresees
    (C) foreseeing
    (D) foresaw

정답) A

해설) 정답은 forseeable임.   in the forseeable future = in the near future 가까운 장래에
    the venture capitalist 벤처 투자가   from his investment 그의 투자로부터
    expects to reap enormous revenue 엄청난 수익을 거둘 것으로 예상하다

158. Santanasoft offers technical support for all of its software products _____ its competitors only provide help for current releases.

    (A) unlike
    (B) whereas
    (C) as far as
    (D) in order that

정답) B

해설) 정답은 whereas임. 문맥상 접속사이고 ~인 반면에 라는 의미의 표현이 와야 하므로
    whereas가 들어가야 함.   as far as~ ~하는 한   in order that~ ~하기 위해서

159. If you want to make your dream come true, you should _____ implement your plans.

    (A) vigilantly
    (B) vigilant
    (C) vigilance
    (D) vigil

정답) A

해설) 정답은 vigilantly임. 조동사와 동사 사이에 들어갈 수 있는 품사는 부사임.

vigilant 자지 않는, 조심스러운   vigilantly 조심스럽게

vigilance 조심, 경계, 불침번   make your dream come true 꿈을 실현하다

160. _____ concerns about rising living cost and monthly rent, the Association of National Housing Policy recommended a sharable house.

(A) Abroad
(B) Atop
(C) Amid
(D) Aside

정답) C

해설) 정답은 Amid임.   Amid~ ~하는 가운데   Aside는 from이 동반되어야 함.

Aside from ~은 별도로 하고   (참고) Apart from~ ~을 제외하고

Amid concerns about rising living cost and monthly rent

오르는 생활비와 월세의 걱정이 있는 가운데

recommend a sharable house 공유할 수 있는 집을 추천하다

161. The owner of Maritime Shipping Inc. announced that the company _____ price of M&A with another corporate.

(A) negotiation
(B) negotiates
(C) negotiability
(D) negotiable

정답) B

해설) 전체 문장의 동사가 없으므로 negotiates가 답임.   negotiate 협상하다

negotiation 협상   negotiability 협상 가능성   negotiable 협상 가능한

M&A = Merger and Acqusition 인수 합병   another corporate 또 다른 회사(법인)

162. Students can _____ access and enroll the professional online study program at the homepage.

(A) easily
(B) least
(C) very
(D) little

정답) A

해설) 정답은 easily임. 조동사와 동사 사이에는 부사가 들어감. easily가 적절함.
easily access 쉽게 접근하다   access 접근, 이용 (명사), 접근하다 (동사)
enroll 등록하다   enrollment 등록

어휘 실력 기르기 28

163. In the newspaper Macrobuilt Inc. announced that it had twelve _____ around the world.

(A) subsidy
(B) subsidiaries
(C) sub
(D) subsidiary

정답) B

해설) 정답은 subsidiaries임.   subsidiary 자회사 (셀 수 있음)   subsidy 보조금
subsidize 보조하다   parent company 모회사임.

164. The billionaire and co-founder of internet messenger program is searching _____ next investment opportunities for the U.S. market.

(A) for
(B) by
(C) at
(D) to

정답) **A**

해설) 정답은 for임. search는 전치사 for를 동반함.   search for~ ~을 찾다
billionaire 억만장자   co-founder 공동 창업자
next investment opportunities 다음 번 투자 기회

165. Ushers at the theater will help the customers _____ their seats especially during the intermission.

(A) make
(B) locate
(C) send
(D) ask

정답) **B**

해설) 정답은 locate임. help + 목적어 + (to)동사원형의 구문임. 의미상 고객들이 자리를 찾는 것을 도와주므로 locate가 적절함.   locate = find
usher (극장 등의) 안내인   especially during the intermission 특히 휴식시간 동안에

166. Magic Purifier co. never turned a profit and the high debt _____ it to default on loans.

(A) made
(B) forced
(C) got
(D) tired

정답) **B**

해설) 정답은 forced임. 회사가 수익을 거두지 못하고 높은 부채로 인해 대출금에 대한 책임 이행을 하지 못했다는 의미이므로 forced가 알맞음.

force + A + to B(부정사) A가 B하도록 강제하다

make + A + B(동사원형) A가 B하도록 시키다(사역동사) 형태도 가능함.

never turned a profit 수익을 내지 못했다   high debt 과도한 빚

forced to default on loans 빚을 갚지 못하도록 만들었다

167. All tickets will be refunded _____ of the bad weather through the homepage of the soccer club.

(A) provided

(B) if

(C) in case of

(D) due

정답) C

해설) 정답은 in case of임. 뒤에 명사구가 뒤따르므로 전치사가 앞에 와야 함.

in case of~ ~하는 경우에 (전치사)   provided that = in case that

All tickets will be refunded in case of~ ~하는 경우에 모든 티켓은 환불된다

168. Many investors purchased the stocks of T&T Inc. despite the _____ that the company's earnings in the first quarter were lower than anticipated.

(A) truth

(B) fact

(C) act

(D) pact

정답) B

해설) 정답은 fact임.   despite the fact that~ that 이하의 사실에도 불구하고

Many investors purchased the stocks of~ 많은 투자자들이 ~의 주식을 매입했다

the company's earnings in the first quarter 1사분기 회사의 수익률

lower than anticipated 예상보다 낮은

169. A year and a half after the launch, the magazine _____ publication due to lack of readers' interest.

   (A) blocked
   (B) stopping
   (C) ceased
   (D) prevented

정답) C

해설) 정답은 ceased임. 선택지에서 stopping이 아니라 stopped이면 정답이 될 수 있음.

cease = stop 멈추다, 그만두다

A year and a half after the launch 출시 후 1년 반 되어서

due to lack of readers' interest 독자의 관심 부족 때문에

170. In the interview with the news press Mark Trumbo's success was mainly _____ on diligence, and passion.

   (A) rely
   (B) based
   (C) come
   (D) stayed

정답) B

해설) 정답은 based임. 문장에서 was가 빠지면 능동태로 rely on도 가능함.

be based on~ ~에 근거를 두다 (수동태)

Mark Trumbo's success was mainly based on diligence, and passion.

= Mark Trumbo's success mainly relied on diligence, and passion.

마크 트럼보의 성공은 주로 부지런함과 열정에 근거했다.

171. The Watertown Prunevill is _____ located just by a metro station which leads to the region's most attractive tourist spot.

(A) conveniently
(B) consistently
(C) continually
(D) commonly

정답) A

해설) 정답은 conveniently임. be located(위치하다) 사이에 부사 conveniently가 들어감.

conveniently 편리하게   consistently 꾸준하게

continually 지속적으로   commonly 일상적으로

lead to the region's most attractive tourist spot 지역에서 가장 매력적인 관광명소로 이끌다

172. You'd better be _____ of the detailed specifications before attempting to install PC vaccine program onto your notebook computer.

(A) direct
(B) review
(C) informed
(D) founded

정답) C

해설) 정답은 be informed of임.   be informed of~ ~에 대해서 정보를 알다

detailed specifications 상세한 설명서   install 설치하다

PC vaccine program PC 백신 프로그램

173. The president's announcement was made during a one-day conference on "Security Research" _____ at the college.

(A) held
(B) hung
(C) kept
(D) seen

정답) A

해설) 정답은 held임. 의미상 대학에서 열린 "안전 연구"에 관한 하루짜리 회담동안에 발표가 이루어졌다는 맥락이므로 held가 정답임.

during a one-day conference on~ ~에 관한 하루짜리 회담에서

the announcement was made 발표가 이루어졌다

174. The host was _____ to announce the last winner of beauty pageant at the Grand Rexington Hall.

(A) delighting
(B) delighted
(C) delights
(D) delight

정답) B

해설) 정답은 delighted임. be delighted to~ ~하게 되어 기쁘다

announce the last winner 최종 승자를 발표하다 beauty pageant 미인대회

어휘 실력 기르기 30

175. With its convenient public transportation and highly skilled workforce, Marion Valley is a very _____ location for IT companies.

(A) offering
(B) proposing
(C) promising
(D) identifying

정답) C

해설) 정답은 promising임. promising 전도유망한 offering 제공하는

proposing 제안하는   identifying 확인하는

promising location for IT companies IT 회사들에 전도유망한 장소

highly skilled workforce 고도로 숙련된 노동력

176. History majors are attending the Metropolitan Museum in New York now that it
_____ authentic Egyptian arts.

(A) feature

(B) features

(C) featureless

(D) featuring

정답) **B**

해설) 정답은 features임.   feature 특집으로 다루다 (동사)

it은 the Metropolitan Museum을 지칭함.

authentic Egyptian arts 진정한 이집트 예술

now that~ that 이하라는 점에서 비슷한 의미의 in that도 가능함.

177. Mr. Crawford is a board member of a nonprofit group _____ the Freedom of the
Reporters.

(A) calls

(B) caller

(C) call

(D) called

정답) **D**

해설) 정답은 called임.   a board of member 이사회 회원   a nonprofit group 비영리 단체
a nonprofit group which is called the Freedom of the Reporters에서 관계대명사와 be
동사가 함께 생략된 것임.

178. The security team will be _____ for the information surveillance by CC TVs from
diverse angles.

(A) response

(B) responsive

(C) respond

(D) responsible

정답) D

해설) 정답은 responsible임.   be responsible for~ ~에 책임을 지다

be responsive to~ = respond to~ ~에 반응하다

information surveillance 정보 감시(감독)   from diverse angles 다양한 각도에서

179. The minister of education has a strong belief that education and learning should be a universal right and not a _____.

(A) privilege

(B) character

(C) reputation

(D) consequence

정답) A

해설) 정답은 privilege임. 문맥상 교육부 장관은 교육과 학습은 보편적인 권리이지 특권이 아니라는 강한 믿음이 있다 라는 해석이므로 빈칸에는 universal right의 상대어인 privilege가 적절함.

180. George Hughes, a famous geneticist who is exploring genetic engineering techniques to _____ extinct species.

(A) revive

(B) survive

(C) involve

(D) revolve

정답) A

해설) 정답은 revive임. 의미상 멸종된 종들을 부활시킨다는 맥락이므로 revive가 적절함.

revive extinct species 멸종된 종들을 복원하다, 부활시키다

survive 살아남다   involve 관련시키다   revolve 회전시키다
geneticist 유전학자   genetic engineering 유전 공학

181. Miller Parkerson had signed over the _____ to his wife just before he experienced the car accident.

    (A) permission
    (B) property
    (C) comparison
    (D) registration

정답) B

해설) 정답은 property임.   sign over property to A 재산을 A에게 양도하다

permission 허락   property 재산   comparison 비교   registration 등록

just before he experienced the car accident 그가 자동차 사고를 겪기 바로 전에

182. The company has not decided _____ how to deal with the unexpected rumors concerning its stocks.

    (A) precise
    (B) precision
    (C) preciseness
    (D) precisely

정답) D

해설) 정답은 precisely임. decide 타동사 다음에 목적어로 how to deal with가 오는 표현이며 3형식의 완전한 문형이므로 사이에는 부사가 들어갈 수 있음.

precise 정밀한, 정확한 precisely 정확하게   precision = preciseness 정밀(성)

how to deal with the unexpected rumors 예상치 못한 루머를 다루는 방법
concerning its stocks 주식에 관하여

183. _____ all the preliminary interviews have been completed, only two applicants for the job opening will be contacted.

   (A) During
   (B) As soon as
   (C) So that
   (D) Despite

정답) B

해설) 정답은 as soon as임. 주어 동사 문장이 빈칸 다음에 나오므로 접속사가 와야 하며 so that은 주절 다음에 목적의 표현에 쓰이므로 의미상 as soon as가 적절함.

As soon as all the preliminary interviews have been completed only two applicants for the job opening will be contacted.

예비 인터뷰가 마무리 되자마자 공석을 위한 두 후보자만 연락이 될 것이다.

184. Chris Bryant and his partner should have consulted a business _____ at the very moment of selling off his company.

   (A) dealer
   (B) party
   (C) adviser
   (D) shopper

정답) C

해설) 정답은 adviser임. 빈칸에 사람의 의미를 나타내는 명사가 적절함.

consult a business advisor 사업 고문에게 자문을 구하다
at the very moment of~ ~하는 바로 그 순간에   sell off 매각하다, 팔다

185. Not only the sales manager but also his CEO was disappointed with sales record _____ the summer vacation season.

(A) while

(B) beside

(C) during

(D) with

정답) B

해설) 정답은 during임.　Not only A but also B = B as well as A A뿐만 아니라 B도

during the summer vacation season 여름휴가 기간 동안에

여름휴가 기간이라는 명사 표현이 나오므로 전치사 during이 쓰이며 만약 빈칸 뒤에 주어와 동사의 문장이 나왔다면 while을 씀.

186. The CEO demanded that the sales manager should give him more _____ ideas on sales promotion.

(A) specifics

(B) specify

(C) specific

(D) specifically

정답) C

해설) 정답은 specific임.　specific ideas 구체적인 아이디어

on sales promotion 매출 촉진에 관한　give A B A에게 B를 주다 (수여동사)

어휘 실력 기르기　32

187. In times of economic boom, price is _____ to increase regardless of pay raise for workers.

(A) risen

(B) seen

(C) limited

(D) bound

정답) D

해설) 정답은 bound임.   be bound to + 동사원형: 반드시 ~하다/~하게 마련이다

In times of economic boom 경제 호황의 시기에

regardless of pay raise for workers 노동자들을 위한 임금 인상에 관계없이

188. According to the Medical News many patients in the U.S. are worried about
_____ in health premiums.

(A) boom

(B) rise

(C) up

(D) upward

정답) B

해설) 정답은 rise임.   rise (명사) = raise 인상   be worried about~ ~을 걱정하다

rise in health premiums 보험료의 인상

189. Based on current customer data, the company prepared for the warranty _____
or complaints.

(A) role

(B) power

(C) claims

(D) pay

정답) C

해설) 정답은 claims임.   warranty claims 보증 청구 (제품에 하자 등이 있을 때 보증서의 약
정 내용을 근거로 청구하는 것)

based on~ ~을 근거로 하여   prepare for~ ~을 준비하다

190. More than 34 percent of the vehicle's owners have filed a _____ against the auto maker regarding the false fuel efficiency.

(A) law
(B) legal
(C) allegation
(D) lawsuit

정답) D

해설) 정답은 lawsuit임. lawsuit = suit 소송 legal 법률의 (형용사), 합법적인 것 (명사) allegation 주장, 진술 file a lawsuit against~ ~에 대해 소송을 걸다
regarding the false fuel efficiency 거짓 연비에 대해서

191. The Business Weekly revealed that the IT company was hesitant to plan to _____ many new employees this year.

(A) recruit
(B) file
(C) join
(D) work

정답) A

해설) recruit가 적절함. recruit 모집하다 reveal that~ that 이하를 폭로하다, 드러내다
file 서류철, 서류철 하다 (참고) file a lawsuit 소송을 제기하다
be hesitant to~ ~하는 데 주저하다

192. If your company wants to be successful in Canada, firstly it has to be developing a major product _____ the market.

(A) leader
(B) leading
(C) leads
(D) lead

정답) B

해설) 시장을 선도할 주요 제품을 개발한다는 의미이므로 leading이 적절함.

a major product (which is) leading the market 시장을 선도하는 주요 제품

a major product와 leading 사이에 관계대명사와 be 동사가 함께 생략된 것임.

어휘 실력 기르기 33

193. Marion & Pamela Cosmetics has announced that its profits this year will be lower due to _____ sales.

    (A) depreciated
    (B) deprived
    (C) determined
    (D) deterred

정답) A

해설) 빈칸에 의미 적절한 형용사를 골라야 하는데 정답은 depreciated임.

depreciated sales 하락한 매출   deprived 박탈당한   determined 결심한

deterred 방해된   deter 방해하다, 저지하다

194. Game companies in the forseeable future should be trying to create more _____ programs for their users.

    (A) invalid
    (B) instinctive
    (C) innovative
    (D) intentional

정답) C

해설) 의미상 사용자들을 위해 혁신적인 프로그램을 창조하도록 노력해야 한다는 맥락이므로 innovative가 정답임.   invalid 유효하지 않은   instinctive 본능적인

innovative 혁신적인   intentional 고의적인   in the forseeable future 가까운 장래에

195. Many IT companies will make 50 to 60% cuts in their work forces _____ the next few years in order to become more competitive.

(A) at
(B) about
(C) over
(D) with

정답) C
해설) over the next few years 다음 몇 년 동안에 걸쳐
    make 50 to 60% cuts in their work forces 노동력의 50%에서 60%를 삭감하다
    in order to become more competitive 더 경쟁력을 갖추기 위해서

196. Many people took into account the fact that solar energy could be a cheap _____ for fossil fuels long time ago.

(A) difference
(B) substitute
(C) replacing
(D) change

정답) B
해설) 정답은 substitute임.   took into account = considered 고려했다
    a cheap substitute for fossil fuels 화석 연료에 대한 값싼 대체재
    long time ago 오래전에

197. The prospect for a good job this year is very _____ according to my professor.

(A) depressive
(B) depressing
(C) depressed
(D) depression

정답) B

해설) 정답은 depressing임. 좋은 직업에 대한 전망이 좋지 못하다는 맥락이므로 depressing을 선택해야 함.   depress 우울하게 만들다   depression 우울증

depressive 우울한, 우울증의

198. The bids for skyscrapers in the heart of Seoul submitted by the construction companies _____ in a special safe.

(A) placing

(B) placed

(C) are placing

(D) were placed

정답) D

해설) 주어가 긴 편이지만 The bids~ companies까지가 주어이다. 의미상으로 수동태가 되어야 하므로 were placed가 적절하다.

in a special safe 특별 금고에 / 여기서 a safe는 금고라는 뜻의 명사이다.

어휘 실력 기르기 34

199. The amusement park is not _____ for any accidents caused by carelessness of children's parents.

(A) respecting

(B) responsible

(C) reasonable

(D) retreating

정답) B

해설) 문맥상 be responsible for~ = be in charge of~ ~에 책임을 지다

respecting 존경하는   reasonable 합리적인   retreating 물러나는
any accidents caused by carelessness of children's parents
아이 부모님들의 부주의로 인한 사고

200. _____ the efforts by the police to reduce criminals and crimes in the region, the results have been disappointing so far.

(A) Although
(B) Despite
(C) In spite
(D) Between

정답) B
해설) 정답은 Despite임.   Despite the efforts 노력에도 불구하고
빈칸 뒤에 명사구가 뒤따르고 있으므로 양보의 의미를 갖는 전치사를 골라야 함.
Despite = in spite of (전치사) ~에도 불구하고
Though = Although = Even though (접속사) ~에도 불구하고
to reduce criminals and crimes 범죄자와 범죄를 줄이기 위해서

201. If you didn't have _____ knowledge of chemistry and physics, you cannot become a professor of military science.

(A) an extensive
(B) an extremely
(C) an outbound
(D) a prevalent

정답) A
해설) 폭넓은 화학 및 물리학 지식이 있어야 한다는 맥락이므로 an extensive가 와야 함.
an extensive knowledge of chemistry and physics 폭넓은 화학과 물리학 지식
extremely 극도로 (부사)   extreme 극단적인 (형용사)
outbound 외부로 가는   prevalent 만연한

202. Many people are _____ to note that a lot of defectors from the North are settling down well in the South.

(A) surprised
(B) surprise
(C) surprises
(D) being surprising

정답) A

해설) 문맥상 surprised가 되어야 함.

be surprised to note that~ that 이하를 알게 되어 놀라다

defector 도주자, 이탈자   settle down 정착하다

be settling down well in the South 남측에서 잘살고 있다

203. High ranking officials in the government is going to have to account _____ the mishandling of the policies.

(A) to
(B) with
(C) for
(D) by

정답) C

해설) account가 명사로 쓰이면 계좌이지만 동사로 쓰이면 for를 동반하여 설명하다 라는 의미를 가짐.   account for~ ~을 설명하다   High ranking officials 고위 관리들 mishandling of the policies 정책의 잘못된 처리, 정책의 실패

204. Due to the severe blizzard the airport _____ announced that it should urgently shut down.

(A) monitors
(B) authorities
(C) party
(D) forces

정답) B
해설) 의미상 심한 눈보라 때문에 공항이 긴급하게 폐쇄한다고 발표했다는 맥락이므로 authorities가 적절함.   authorities 당국 (항상 복수 형태임)   authority 권위
Due to the severe blizzard 심한 눈보라 때문에

어휘 실력 기르기 35

205. The managing director could not set up a _____ plan on how many products should be churned out.

(A) reasoning
(B) reasons
(C) reason
(D) reasonable

정답) D
해설) 관사와 명사 사이에 빈칸이 있으므로 의미 적절한 형용사가 들어가야 함.
reasonable 합리적인   reasoning 추론의, 이성의   reason 이유, 이성
managing director 전무이사   churn out = produce 생산하다
set up a reasonable plan 합리적인 계획을 세우다

206. The delivery order was _____ a year after the Jackson Vill Food Inc. and its contractor re-established business relations.

(A) send
(B) made
(C) went
(D) transmitted

정답) B

해설) 정답은 made임. make an order에서 수동태 표현이 된 것임.

The delivery order was made 배달 주문이 일어났다   contractor 하청업체, 계약업체

re-establish business relations 사업 관계를 재설정하다

207. The managing director in Meter & Miles Corporation _____ with its counterpart on details of sales condition between two companies.

    (A) recommends

    (B) negotiates

    (C) refers

    (D) consults

정답) B

해설) 정답은 negotiate임.   negotiate with~ ~와 협상하다   refer to 언급하다, 참조하다

recommend 추천하다 (뒤에 목적어를 바로 쓰는 타동사임)   consult 참조하다 (타동사)

negotiate with its counterpart 상대자와 협상하다

on details of sales condition 영업 조건의 세부사항에 관하여

208. The number of diesel cars on the road _____ increasing due to cheap fuel and fuel efficiency.

    (A) are

    (B) are being

    (C) is

    (D) is been

정답) C

해설) 단수 취급하기 때문에 단수동사가 옴.   The number of~ ~의 숫자

A number of = many의 뜻이므로 뒤에 항상 복수동사가 쓰임.

due to cheap fuel and fuel efficiency 싼 연료와 연료 효율 때문에

209. Thanks to the trip-cancellation policy, he could get a _____ on his air fare from the insurance company.

(A) bill

(B) money

(C) refund

(D) premium

정답) C

해설) 문맥상 환불받는다는 내용이 적절하므로 refund가 정답임.

get a refund on~ ~에 대해 환불받다

Thanks to the trip-cancellation policy 여행취소 약관 때문에

he could get a refund on his air fare 그는 항공 요금 환불을 받을 수 있었다

210. Whether you're traveling domestically or _____, a travel insurance is necessary for yourself.

(A) apart

(B) anytime

(C) alone

(D) abroad

정답) D

해설) 문맥상 or를 중심으로 대칭 형태이므로 abroad가 정답임.

domestically or aborad 국내로 혹은 해외로

be necessary for~ ~을 위해 필요하다   for yourself 당신 자신을 위해

지은이 **조동인**

외대 영어과 졸
뉴욕주립대 석사 졸
외대 영문학 박사 졸
현, 인하공전 항공운항과 교수

Vitamin New Toeic Voca

발행일 2016년 8월 29일
지은이 조동인 **발행인** 이성모
발행처 도서출판 동인 / 서울시 종로구 혜화로3길 5 118호
등 록 1-1599호
전 화 (02)765-7145 **팩스** (02)765-7165
이메일 dongin60@chol.com

ISBN 978-89-5506-724-8 **정가** 12,000원

※ 잘못 만들어진 책은 바꾸어 드립니다.